Praise for

How to Grow a Young Music Lover

"Why leave such a powerful and pleasurable legacy as your child's experience of music to whatever happens to be on the radio? Cheri Fuller knows better. She helps you reach for the possibilities of rearing a lifelong music lover."
> —DAVID KOPP, *founding editor of* Christian Parenting Today
> *magazine and author of numerous books, including*
> Praying the Bible for Your Children

"In *How to Grow a Young Music Lover,* Cheri Fuller beautifully communicates that music is a wonderful treasure, a gift from God, and a legacy that must be passed on to future generations."
> —CHRISTOPHER PARKENING, *classical guitarist and recording artist*

"*How to Grow a Young Music Lover* provides encouraging practical suggestions for parents or teachers hoping to see their child succeed in music. Even those families who feel they are 'nonmusical' can benefit from her insights. I highly recommend this book."
> —MARY RICE HOPKINS *(www.maryricehopkins.com), recording artist,*
> *composer, author, and mother*

"This book is full of ideas for integrating music into the life of children from infancy through the teen years. The discussion of music-education methods gives parents an overview to use as a guide in making decisions about music experiences for their children."
> —MARY HOPPER, *professor of choral music,*
> *Wheaton Conservatory of Music*

"Cheri Fuller's book is a must-read for all parents who want to make music part of family life. As an educator and parent, I know firsthand the part that music plays in the intellectual development of children. It isn't just an extra. It's a necessity."

—ELAINE MCEWAN, *author of numerous books, including* Attention Deficit Disorder *and* Ten Traits of Highly Successful Schools

"Having nine very musical children of our own, my wife and I have found *How to Grow a Young Music Lover* to be one of the most valuable resources we've ever come across. If you would like to hear your home filled with music and if you want your child to understand that the greatest purpose of music is to express love for God, this book is for you. An excellent tool for home-schoolers or classroom teachers, this resource is a godsend for anyone who desires to nurture a well-rounded love of music in a child."

—DENNIS JERNIGAN, *worship leader, author, and recording artist with Here to Him Music*

How to
Grow a Young
MUSIC LOVER

How to
Grow a Young
MUSIC LOVER

Helping Your Child Discover and Enjoy the World of Music

Cheri Fuller

Foreword by Charlie Peacock

WATERBROOK
PRESS

HOW TO GROW A YOUNG MUSIC LOVER

All Scripture quotations, unless otherwise indicated, are taken from the *Holy Bible, New International Version*®. NIV®. Copyright © 1973, 1978, 1984 by International Bible Society. Used by permission of Zondervan Publishing House. All rights reserved. Scripture quotations marked (KJV) are taken from the *King James Version*.

Trade Paperback ISBN 978-0-87788-370-8

Published in the United States by WaterBrook, an imprint of the Crown Publishing Group, a division of Penguin Random House LLC, New York.

WATERBROOK® and its deer colophon are registered trademarks of Penguin Random House LLC.

Library of Congress Cataloging-in-Publication Data
Fuller, Cheri.
    How to grow a young music lover : helping your child discover and enjoy the world of music / Cheri Fuller.
        p. cm.
    Includes bibliographical references, discography, and lists of video cassettes and computer software.
    ISBN 0-87788-370-X
    1. Music—Instruction and study—Juvenile. 2. Music appreciation—Juvenile. 3. Education—Parent participation.
    I. Title.
    MT6.F79H7 1994
    780—dc20   93-10877
                                                                                                          CIP
                                                                                                          MN

Printed in the United States of America
2017
10 9 8 7 6 5 4

To my grandchildren

Caitlin Elizabeth Fuller
Caleb Cole Fuller
Noah Christopher Plum
Josephine Bryce Fuller

Contents

PART FOUR: RESOURCES

Foreword

Part of my work is to dream good dreams for music. As a Christian and a musician, I'm one among many appointed to steward the music of the past, present, and future—yes, even music that has yet to be conceptualized or heard. Each day I ask, and hopefully answer, a foundational question: What does it mean to love God, his church, and the watching world through music? I'm up early doing this work whether there's a high degree of public interest or not! It's what I do. Oh, but to be able to do this work in a heart, a church, or a culture that is prepared to listen, where music is valued, understood, and even championed—that is the dream, the hope of every musician. It's a worthy one, even godly.

After reading this wonderful book on growing young music lovers, I am certain Cheri Fuller is about the business of making my dream come true! Thank you, Cheri. She wants to help the human family fill the world with people who love music, who know why they love it, and who grow up to replicate this truth and passion in generations to follow. This is a beautiful goal. If her dream comes true, there'll be plenty of discerning listeners for those of us who make the music of the past, present, and future. Moreover, some portion of these young music lovers will grow up to become the music makers of the future—men and women who will steward the ideas of the past, but also dream new dreams for music's future.

No less important will be the presence of people in the church and the world who love music because God loves music. They will be the schoolteachers, lawyers, homemakers, copy editors, and heavy-equipment operators who remember the words of Zephaniah 3:17, "The LORD your God is with you, he is mighty to save. He will take great delight in you, he will quiet you with his love, he will rejoice over you with singing."

Those who follow and serve the God Who Sings take the stewardship of music and young hearts very seriously. It's what the family of God does. But it's a calling that plays itself out within the multitude of individual families that make up the huge human family throughout history. Cheri wisely understands this, and so begins her book with the subject of music and the family. The family is where every child's musical journey ought to begin. Parents, that's not your cue to start feeling inadequate to the task. As Cheri makes clear, parental musical expertise is not a necessary ingredient in growing young music lovers. A love of music grows out of the enjoyment and simple use of music in a variety of cultural settings, not in the learning of musical scales or memorizing the birth dates of classical composers. While an in-depth musical education would likely include such things, a true, transforming musical education always begins with the embodiment of good, that is, listening to and enjoying music and making it in the simplest of ways. This is something all parents can give their children.

Need more direction? Start here: Live the life of the new way to be human as modeled by Jesus; enjoy and use music in a diversity of ways; discover and rediscover all kinds of music and share it with your little ones. This is the approach my wife and I took with our own children, now young adults contributing their own musical story to the church and the world.

In the words of our daughter, Molly Nicholas: "It's often said that children learn most by observing what their parents do. I would have to say that this holds true in encouraging my love of music. Growing up with a parent who is a musician, I was often in recording studios, at concerts, or in my living room hearing songs being written. But even more than the obvious factor of my dad's career, I would say that my love of music was influenced by the albums my parents listened to. Sting's *Dream of the Blue Turtles,* Paul Simon's *Graceland,* most anything by James Taylor or the Beatles. This was music. There was a consistent element of creativity and innovation, yet a knowledge that this music was classic and would stand (or had stood) the test of time. Case in point: In 1987, when we went to the electronics store and bought our first CD player, my parents picked out two CDs to start off our collection: Miles Davis's *Kind of Blue* and Peter Gabriel's *So.* With each new melody, new song, and new album, I was, and still continue to be, awakened to a more complete picture of what music can be."

This is the goal in all of life. Isn't the history of redemption an incremental unfolding of a more complete picture of what life can, should, and will be—including music?

Our son, Sam Ashworth, remembers living "in a home full of music. I had so many classic records at my disposal. I remember being as young as six and listening to Beatles albums one after the other. It's roots like these that make a kid grow up to love and strive for creativity and originality."

What we listen to, how we use music, what we say about it, and how curious we are with respect to it, all teach our children something about music.

Hopefully Molly and Sam learned to respect the diversity of music made in the past and in their own present, freeing them up to use and enjoy music in new and diverse ways in the future. To encourage this good outcome, they were exposed to Keith Jarrett's piano improvisations, Maranatha Music's Psalty, Glenn Gould's Bach interpretations, Victoria Williams, King Sunny Adé, John Coltrane, Phil Keaggy, Amy Grant, and yes, the Beatles, just to name a few. We wanted Molly and Sam to leave our home prepared with a big view of the use and enjoyment of music. We wanted them to love music because God loves music and has graciously allowed it to be a part of life's tapestry now and in the new heaven and earth to come. We dreamed of our children being vital contributors to the ongoing musical story, people who know how to love God, his church, and the watching world through music.

As I've written elsewhere, "Music is the soundtrack to the story we're telling through our lives and our communities. Through emotion and word it documents our journey. It looks back at past grace and in gratitude gives God worshipful praise. It looks forward in faith to future grace and gives God praise as well. Music is present when we're born and when we're buried, when we learn our ABCs and when we graduate from high school, when we celebrate birthdays, baptisms, Christmas and Easter, when we first hear the gospel, when we share our first dance, our first kiss, and when we marry. Music is both a quiet song in our hearts and a thundering symphony that takes our breath away. Our enjoyment and use of it seems to know no end. It is literally the sonic backdrop to life and culture. All in all, it's possible to say that music is everywhere and not risk exaggeration."[1]

If this is true, shouldn't we who serve the God Who Sings commit to growing music lovers who'll one day enter the everywhere and everything of life as God's direct representatives?

Absolutely. We can be grateful that Cheri Fuller has taken the time to encourage us and equip us for such a noble effort. May the God Who Sings use this book to his everlasting glory.

—Charlie Peacock-Ashworth, musician,
recording artist, and author

Preface

During the writing of the first edition of *How to Grow a Young Music Lover,* our three children were still at home. Now they are married and parents themselves, affording us the delight of seeing the love and enjoyment that our grandchildren, Caitlin, Caleb, and Noah, gain from music.

My daughter-in-law Tiffany was on the worship team throughout her pregnancy, so Caitlin, now age three, was surrounded by praise and worship music for nine months before she was even born. When she was only a few weeks old, Caitlin showed a strong preference for certain worship music. If she was fussy and Tiffany played a Harry Connick, Donut Man, or Phish CD, the music had little calming effect. But when Tiffany played "Holy Is the Lord," Caitlin was instantly soothed. By the time she was six months old, she was singing along with her unique melody when we sang "You Are My Sunshine" or "Jesus Loves the Little Children." Her little brother, Caleb, now one, drums to the music with quite a regular beat. And Noah Christopher smiles at me with a distinct look of recognition when I sing to him "Jesus Loves Me" (a favorite song I sing to our grandchildren). He likes to sit on his mom's lap while she plays the piano. Noah kicks his "piano" on the end of his crib and chooses tunes at only five months. And when baby Josephine is born in a few months, she will be surrounded by wonderful music. Even now she is probably tapping her little foot in utero as her daddy plays his guitar.

As Caitlin, Caleb, Noah, and Josephine show us, children respond to the rhythm and sound of music from the earliest years. We also know that children can benefit from a variety of musical activities, like piano or violin lessons, and from participating in group music activities, like choir and band. In the first edition of this book, I discussed ways that music participation and listening (especially to classical music) enhance children's education.

But since the first version of *How to Grow a Young Music Lover* was published several years ago, there has been even more research concerning the positive, powerful effects of music on the brain development and learning capacities of babies and young children. New high-tech brain imaging methods such as PET scan (positron emission tomography) and MRI (magnetic resonance imaging) allow researchers to see which parts of the child's brain are stimulated during different activities and to understand the amazing ways that music affects the brain's "wiring" or development.

Not only does music have brain-boosting benefits, it also nurtures the emotional and spiritual life of a child. Music is a gift for a lifetime—a gift that we have the chance to introduce to our children. But it's between birth and about age nine or ten when children are most sensitive and receptive to music. We call this season of life the "Musical Window," because every time a child in that age range has a musical experience, a "mapping" goes on in the brain. In that mapping, one neuron connects to another and then another, laying down "tracks" on which the "train" of musical behaviors and skills will be able to run for the rest of a person's life. The more musical experiences kids have, the more "track" they have.

With all the responsibilities of diapering and feeding our children, helping them succeed in education and sports, and balancing our household tasks, family life, jobs, church, and community activities, we can let life zoom by, devoting little time to what is truly important. Yet music is one of those essential parts of childhood that we don't want our children to miss.

I'm delighted to offer this book for a new generation of parents. It is my hope that this new edition of *How to Grow a Young Music Lover* will inspire your heart with a wealth of ideas and resources to make music not only an enriching facet of your child's development but part of the rhythm of your family life. As you explore and enjoy music together, may it enrich your relationships and provide many happy memories. And as your kids grow up with music, may they each develop unique ways to express their creativity that will build their sense of self-worth, provide something to give to others, contribute to their own joy and success in living and learning for a lifetime—and most of all, glorify God.

Acknowledgments

I want to thank those parents and teachers who shared their musical background, their love for music, and their suggestions with me, especially Robin Wolaver, Posy Lough, Carolyn Nystrom, Dianne Phillips, Penny Hook, Mary Carr, and Dr. John Feierabend. Thank you to Patty Johnston and Flo Perkins for their prayers and to Cathy Kelsay for computer support. A special thank-you to my editor, Ramona Tucker, for her patience and enthusiasm about this project and to the entire staff at Harold Shaw, and to Elisa Fryling and Carol Bartley, editors of the new edition, and the folks at WaterBrook Press.

I am always grateful to Holmes, my husband, for his belief in me, his love, and his faithful support, and to our children and grandchildren, who keep a song in my heart.

Most of all, I thank Marilyn Rosfeld, Doctor of Musical Arts, Piano Performance and Pedagogy, and Adjunct Professor at Oklahoma City University, for her expert consulting, for her contributions and suggestions throughout, and especially for "Classics Month-by-Month," information on musical games and hymns, and "A Parent and Teacher's Guide to Music Resources."

Part One

Music and Your Family

Chapter One

Music: A Form of Remembering

Music is…a form of remembering,
a return to the seasons of the heart, long ago.

MENOTTI

Music marked important times in my childhood: carols sung at Christmas and majestic hymns at Easter, birthday party singing, patriotic songs on the first day of elementary school, playing "Name That Tune" to pass the time while traveling on the train to see my grandma in Houston, songs we learned at church camp. Music was a happy part of life in the Heath household. Neither of my parents was a musician. Mama never felt she had a good voice, but she enthusiastically sang the hymns at church and hummed little melodies as she cooked and sewed. Papa loved music and sang to us from the time we were babies.

We didn't have an expensive stereo or sound equipment. We had an old jukebox that played children's records, Burl Ives's songs, Patti Page and Eddie Arnold records, and big-band music. As soon as I could talk, I was singing along with the jukebox and chiming in on songs with my big sisters. We sang jingles and rhymes as we jumped rope outside and played musical chairs at parties (someone was always having a birthday, it seemed). Singing made our steps lighter as we walked to school. Mother didn't drive, so we got in lots of walking, chanting, and marching as the blocks melted away. We banged away on the old piano in the living room, where early I learned to play by ear "Chopsticks," "Blue Moon," and other easy favorites.

When I was six years old, Papa asked if I would like to learn to play the guitar. It sounded like great fun to be included with the three big girls (as my older sisters were called) and get to play an instrument. So Papa took us every week to Johnny Giles's house in Dallas, where the four of us received music lessons—on guitars, piano, and accordion. From then on we played our instruments and sang together as a little band at home for Papa's enjoyment, songs like "Tennessee Waltz" (his favorite), "Yellow Rose of Texas," and many others. We played at church and for missions in inner-city Dallas and once on the big stage at the State Fair of Texas. For that event, Mom even made us matching costumes.

I was able to take guitar lessons for only three years because Papa died, but that foundational instruction has kept me playing guitar for the rest of my life. I've never been what I would call accomplished, but I could accompany my children's singing in their growing-up years and could play for the Sunday school classes I taught. (Children are very forgiving and patient with our lack of musical skill—they just enjoy a live instrument!) What fun it was to make music together.

Music is a wonderful treasure that can last a lifetime and be passed on to future generations. It is a gift to our children and grandchildren, a legacy that often lasts much longer than many of the other activities and entertainment we provide. When our daughter Alison was in high school, she picked up my guitar one summer, after several years of piano, and began to practice chords. She taught herself to play, set aside times to practice, and began to accompany and lead worship at her Sunday night youth group, youth retreats, and other gatherings. What a joy to see the songs go on!

The hymns and choruses I learned as a child in Sunday school and church, Vacation Bible School, and church camps were valuable for another important reason—they helped form the core of my theology, the foundations of my faith. I learned that Christ is the only Solid Rock and that building my life on anything else is like standing on sinking sand, that Jesus loves me because the Bible tells me so, that I can truly carry everything to him in prayer, and that Christ is the best friend I could ever have. Through music I discovered early in life that I can surrender all to God and have him guide my life, that there really is victory in Jesus for whatever challenges I face, and that someday when this life is over, I'll fly away to heaven and be with him forever. And in the meantime, I can face tomorrow because he lives!

The old, wonderful hymns are part of the fabric of my memories—all six of us children and Mom in the pew of our Baptist church, singing and worshiping God—and their truths sustained me through years of teenage doubts, tragedies in our family, and the inevitable jolts of life until my relationship with God was renewed in my late twenties. Then the familiar words rang with new life and meaning.

Music is…love in search of a word.—Whittier

Music became especially important to me in the summer of 1982 when my mother was dying of cancer. I saw the incredible comfort and strength she derived from our singing scriptures:

> Beauty for ashes, the oil of joy for mourning, the garment of
> praise for the spirit of heaviness; that they might be called trees
> of righteousness, the planting of the LORD, that he might be
> glorified. (Isaiah 61:3, KJV)

As my sisters and I sat around Mom's bed at Baylor Hospital and held her hand, we sang to her the hymns and songs we'd sung as young girls. Life was coming full circle. Comfort and love flowed as we sang harmony on "Amazing Grace," "This Is My Story," and "Blessed Assurance." Our voices blended and harmonized although we hadn't sung together for several years.

Music was a joy to me when I was a young mother. When Justin, Chris, and Alison were babies and I nursed and rocked them in the old yellow rocker, I sang to them my songs of childhood—silly rhyming songs, soothing lullabies, and songs of faith. Then as they grew, music continued to form a pleasant backdrop of our family life. Hearing cassette recordings from the fictitious place called Agapeland, songs from *Antsylvania* and the Psalty series, and other kid stuff was a regular part of running errands in the car. We listened to everything from dulcimer and folk music, classical guitar recordings, and John Michael Talbot (Christian guitarist and gifted singer) to Beethoven's Fifth Symphony. I always preferred to have music playing through our house than have the television on while I worked and the children played nearby.

Every day that is born into this world
comes like a burst of music…
and thou shalt make of it a dance, a dirge,
or a life march, as thou wilt.—Thomas Carlyle

I admit to being a veteran whistler (much to my daughter's chagrin when she was a teenager—"Mom, it's embarrassing for you to whistle or hum in the grocery store!"). I whistled when I walked our shelty, Lady, down the lane or worked alone in the kitchen. Did you know it's hard to whistle and stay in a bad mood?

Sometimes I got out my guitar and we sang together "Old MacDonald Had a Farm," "I Had a Little Rooster by the Barnyard Gate," "Froggy Went a Courtin'," or "You Are My Sunshine," while the children played rhythm instruments. And they loved to have "family church time" when we would sing praise and Scripture songs. In all of these early experiences at home, good seeds were planted for lifelong enjoyment of music.

We've also found that music bridges the cultures. When two girls from Bunko University in Japan stayed with us, they wanted to learn to speak English better; they could write it but had limited conversation skills. It took lots of gesturing and guessing to bridge the gap between our different languages and culture. But one evening I wrote out the words to some American songs. Playing the guitars, we taught them several traditional tunes. As their smiles grew broader and they sang out, their confidence in their English skills increased. The next night they practiced their new American songs and committed several to memory. They taught us a Japanese song and sang some of their favorites for us. We made tapes of our singing together, which they took back to Japan—to practice, they said!

> *Music is God's best gift to man,*
> *the only art of heaven given to earth,*
> *and the only art of earth that we can take to heaven.*
> *—Charles Landon*

Music is not just a gift for us to enjoy ourselves but a gift we can give back to God again and again—and that further increases his and our joy. With music we can lift our hearts to praise and worship him, for "Great is the LORD, and most worthy of praise," as Psalm 48:1 says. We can join with the heavens and the angels to proclaim his faithfulness and majesty:

> The heavens declare the glory of God;
>   the skies proclaim the work of his hands.
> Day after day they pour forth speech;
>   night after night they display knowledge.

> There is no speech or language
>> where their voice is not heard.
> Their voice goes out into all the earth,
>> their words to the ends of the world. (Psalm 19:1-4)

With our voices, with instruments, with our hands clapping, with dance, even with a "loud timbrel," we praise the God of the universe. As a result we find our own hearts lifted up and inspired, our perspective about problems and stresses broadened, and our minds and lives renewed. As Berthold Auerbach, a nineteenth-century German novelist, said, "Music washes away from the soul the dust of everyday life."

When we sing to God, an amazing transference takes place: God instructs us, comforts us, inspires us, and assures us of his love. He is even singing over us! As Zephaniah 3:17 says, "The LORD your God is with you, he is mighty to save. He will take great delight in you, he will quiet you with his love, he will rejoice over you with singing."

Classical music provides a rich heritage for broadening musical horizons. Even babies and children appreciate the dynamics, emotions, and intelligence of classical music; it enriches and nourishes their lives, accelerates their learning, and enhances brain development, as you'll read about in the chapters ahead. So I've included a "Classics Month-by-Month" (chapter 10) through which you and your family can explore together classical music composers and their pieces that children especially enjoy.

In "Your Child's Musical Development" (chapter 4), I've described the characteristics of each age and suggested activities and ideas to enrich your child's musical experience. In "Learning to Make Music" (chapter 5), you'll find ways to encourage your child's growth in the study of piano, violin, or any instrument. We'll look at how to deal with the music of popular culture (including the culture of teenagers!) in chapter 8. There is also a guide to hymns (chapter 9) and one for music games and activities (chapter 6). We'll explore "The Joy of Movement" in chapter 7. And the resource sections of individual chapters, along with the appendices, list and describe many suggested books, recordings, and videos for the whole family. My hope is that with this book you can help your child discover and enjoy the world of music.

Chapter Two

The Joys and Benefits
of Music Making

Music is ecstasy, a heart leaping, an explosion of God's joy.

ANONYMOUS

Music making is one of the real joys in life, and children can benefit from a variety of musical activities. The sheer delight of children's singing and playing, listening to fine music, dancing, playing a musical instrument, and enjoying music as a family is a reward in itself. But music making and early musical training also offer tremendous benefits for your child—academically, emotionally, socially, and spiritually.

MUSIC FOR MUSIC'S SAKE

Before we talk about how music benefits a child's cognitive, motor, or creative development, let's look at the tremendous value and importance of music just for music's sake. As Dr. John Feierabend, director of education at the Hartt School of Music in Hartford, Connecticut, says, "Music in early childhood develops lifelong abilities and sensitivities which enrich everyday life for all people. Neglect of that development in early childhood causes an irreversible loss of that potential."

Music brings a richness to our experience—a wonder, joy, and beauty that nothing else can. Even if it didn't bring all the "extramusical" benefits of social, physical, and intellectual development that follow in this chapter, music is a valuable part of our lives for its own sake. Our spirit can be lifted, our perspective heightened, our emotions comforted or cheered—all because of an instrumental, a hymn, or a song that touches us at several levels. Music can make us feel a range of emotions. It brings back memories—of our wedding long ago, a special family Christmas gathering, or a play our child was in. If we can't tune in to music, one of life's best joys is lost.

Our society assumes certain musical behaviors from all of us throughout our adult lives:

> We are expected to dance at weddings, cheer at sporting events while clapping hands in time with the crowd, sing "Happy Birthday" to friends and relatives, or share a lullaby with an infant. Although all people should have those minimum musical competencies, some will be more deeply involved with music as consumers of recorded and live music, while others will become performing musicians. Regardless of our ultimate level of involvement with music, the success of our musical experiences may depend on the musical nurturing we received during our preschool years.[1]

Feierabend and other experts believe that exposure to and involvement with music in the early years actually determine one's ability to hear and distinguish different tones and rhythms and develop the sensitivity to different types of music as well as the capacity to appreciate and enjoy music.

Unfortunately, many children today arrive at school not knowing the singing games and rhymes children used to know, lacking skills in making music, and unable to sing well and move rhythmically to music. In addition, many kids are missing out on the wonderful interaction between themselves and adults that can come through music.

Feierabend suggests that children deprived of music experiences in the first critical years of their lives become "music-blind," unable to perceive the beauty that music can bring to them, just as a person who is color-blind is not able to distinguish between certain basic colors and appreciate the spectrum of colors that exist in the world.

Children who grow up in families where they hear music, are sung to, and get to move and sing develop a much greater sensitivity to hear and respond to music. Dr. Edwin Gordon, formerly a professor at Temple University, defines music aptitude as *audiation,* the ability to retain a short melody "in your mind" (or to hear music that is not physically present), and distinguish and retain tonal and rhythmic patterns. Gordon discovered through his research that music audiation abilities decline if the child did not receive musical stimulation.[2]

Just as there are periods of readiness for developing reading or other skills, there are critical periods in musical development, especially for acquiring the tools to mentally retain tonal or rhythmic patterns. The first three years are the most critical for musical stimulation, a time when you should be singing and dancing with your child—Mother Goose rhymes, "patty caking," lullabies— listening to the best recorded music, and playing musical games. Each year after that is critical, but the effect on nurturing the musical aptitude is a little less than the previous year, until age nine when audiation stabilizes. How clearly you are able to hear and respond to tunes at age nine is approximately the same as how clearly you're able to hear tunes as a grownup.[3]

> *Music helps the child to discover beauty. Children's eyes are very sensitive to bright and beautiful colors. We should also develop their sensitivity to beautiful musical sounds.*—Unknown

Children assimilate music in much the same way they learn language during their first five years of life, so it is important that music and movement be blended into their daily routine in those early years (regardless of their lack of coordination in moving or skill in singing).

Whatever children experience musically at school and church is good. But the best—the most natural and valuable music enrichment—should come from a child's home. Feierabend and other experts agree on this. If you don't know any children's songs or folk songs, get a recording and learn some! (See appendix B: "A Parent's and Teacher's Guide to Music Resources" for suggestions.) If you used to play an instrument, get it out, dust it off, and practice some favorite songs you sang as a child. If you don't know much about classical music, you can learn along with your children with "Classics Month-by-Month" (chapter 10). There you will have a composer of the month to introduce to your child, listen to his selected classical music, learn some musical terms, and play the game that is suggested.

We know that the broader the repertoire of music the child listens to and the richer his home music environment, the higher will be the child's intuitive understanding of how music is organized and the more clearly he will be able to hear music, learn to play instruments, and appreciate music throughout his entire life.

MUSIC AS PRELANGUAGE

Now let's look at the many ways music making, listening, and training enrich a child's life. Research indicates that music participation significantly boosts children's general achievement and aptitude. According to researchers at the University of California at Irvine (UCI), musical training for children may help them strike a higher note when it comes to overall mental ability. It is known through many research studies that infants recognize and respond to music, and the UCI scientists believe that is because humans are born with certain brain cells that respond to musical sounds.

Just as there can be no music without learning,
no education is complete without music.
Music makes the difference.—Unknown

Physicist Gordon Shaw says that these neurons work in patterns that can be expanded as a sort of prelanguage to perform increasingly complex inter-actions—even before the brain has developed verbal language skills. This ability may bolster higher-level thinking skills. In fact, experts believe that music par-ticipation and training at an early age are some of the best "exercises" for devel-oping logical and sequential thinking and higher cognitive abilities that boost achievement in math and science.[4]

MUSIC STRENGTHENS MEMORY

How many of us first could say the entire alphabet from learning to sing the "ABC" song? Can you remember specific verses from the Bible because they have been set to music and you've learned them as choruses? From recalling jingles on television commercials to memorizing their ABCs, children learn an enormous amount of information with the help of music.

Music is a right-brained function, and speech and language are left-brained functions. So that's why music combined with words (Scripture verses set to music, for instance) aids the listener in remembering the words. In fact, words learned in this fashion go into your long-term memory and can be retrieved years later even if you haven't practiced the information.

If your child enjoys music, use it to maximize homework and study time. Help your child make up a song for learning the U.S. states and capitals or the multiplication tables. Music makes learning more fun and strengthens memory skills.

MUSIC AND SCHOOL ACHIEVEMENT

Early, positive musical experiences are very important for children. Studying, listening to, and practicing music enhance the social, cognitive, motor, affective, and creative development of the child, while providing sheer enjoyment. They also boost the concentration and memory skills needed for school success.

According to Mary Carr, a piano teacher from Yarmouth, Maine, for over thirty years, "Music study fortifies all the learning—in reading, math, and other subjects—that children are doing at school." It also helps language and communication skills develop and even paves the way for the mastery of foreign languages. As children grow, musical training continues to help them develop the discipline and self-confidence to achieve in school. The day-to-day practice, along with setting goals and reaching them, develops self-discipline, patience, and persistence. That discipline carries over to other areas, such as doing homework and other school projects responsibly and on time and keeping materials organized.

Music aids in the development of visual, auditory, and language skills. It also develops hand, ear, and eye coordination and improves agility, dexterity, and small muscle development. In addition, the attention span is lengthened. Perhaps that is why a recent report by the Rockefeller Foundation stated that musical kids are more likely to get to college and be successful there. When children study music, they enhance their overall academic skills.

> *Music speaks what cannot be expressed*
> *Soothes the mind and gives it rest*
> *Heals the heart and makes it whole*
> *Flows from heaven to the soul.—Anonymous*

Over a two-year period, students who were enrolled in music courses scored an average of twenty to forty points higher on both the verbal and math portions of the SAT (Scholastic Aptitude Test). This same research showed that students who participate in their school orchestra or band are 52 percent more likely to go on to college and graduate. So, as Dr. Frank Wilson says, "Involving your child in musical activities at an early age is really kind of an investment in his or her future."[5]

MUSIC AND MEDICINE

Music is a soother, both physically and emotionally, and mounting medical evidence is confirming music's amazing power to heal. Researchers at the UCLA School of Nursing in Los Angeles and at Georgia Baptist Medical Center in Atlanta found that premature babies gained weight faster, were able to use oxygen more efficiently, and were released from neonatal intensive care nurseries much earlier when they listened to soothing music mixed with voices or womb sounds.

Researchers and doctors have found that listening to classical music reduced critical care patients' need for sleeping pills and pain medication and speeded their recovery. Some studies indicate that music lessens physiological responses to stress and helps the body increase the production of endorphins (natural pain relievers) and enzymes that speed healing and reduce the danger of infection.[6]

Music therapy—such as having a quick lesson on a portable keyboard and then playing and singing together with a therapist or in a group with other kids—is also helping young cancer patients communicate about and cope with their treatments.

SPIRITUAL BENEFITS

"For months I was severely depressed," said a friend recently. "I was in total despair, even suicidal. I tried to read my Bible but couldn't; I couldn't even pray." But she could sing—and she found that when she did, the oppressive feelings were chased away; it was the only thing that brought relief.

> *Day by day and with each passing moment,*
> *Strength I find to meet my trials here;*
> *Trusting in my Father's wise bestowment,*
> *I've no cause for worry or for fear.*
> *—Lina Sandell, "Day by Day"*

Singing songs such as "Jesus Loves Me" and "Jesus...There's Just Something About That Name" helped this depressed friend shift her focus to God instead of her heavy burdens and dark feelings. She expressed extreme gratitude that as a child she had been taught hundreds of hymns and choruses and was able to recall them at her time of need.

Here are other benefits of "making music to the Lord":

- It lifts our spirits and redirects our minds from earthly burdens and hassles; this helps us regain a hopeful perspective by focusing on God and not ourselves. Choruses like "Wonderful Counselor" give us a way to praise God for who he is—"Almighty God, Everlasting Father, Jesus, Our Emmanuel, We Adore Thee…"

- It imparts to children values such as love, understanding, obedience, and compassion and shows them the importance of God's Word and work in our lives. There's a wealth of outstanding Christian contemporary music for kids that builds strong biblical values (see appendix B).

- It gives children resources that help them cope with many different situations and challenges in life.

- Singing "psalms, hymns and spiritual songs" as Colossians 3:16 says—whether that is contemporary praise and worship music, gospel songs, or hymns, is a form of worship that cannot be replaced. As the song says, wherever you go, you can "take the name of Jesus with you," while driving, showering, working, cooking, or even going to sleep. Choruses and hymns can become a part of your entire being—internalized, forever music in your heart.

> *God is its author, and not man;*
> *he laid the keynote of all harmonies;*
> *he planned all perfect combinations, and he made us*
> *so that we could hear and understand.—Anonymous*

EMOTIONAL BENEFITS

Music also relieves anxiety, tension, and depression. You can listen to music while you're doing any number of things. It helps ease the strain of difficult days, calm you down, or energize you, depending on what type of music you're listening to. "Music helps me relax when I'm upset, gives me insights into the Christian life, and gives me a feeling of peace," said Angela, a fourteen-year-old who studies voice and piano.

"When you've quiet music playing, it provides a sense of peace and serenity and comfort when there's turmoil," says Diane, a minister of children's music. "While growing up in a dysfunctional family, music had a very calming effect on me. It helped me cope, providing inspiration and a sense of refuge from the storm." Although her family wasn't interested or involved in music, they did support her involvement and allowed her to build her own record collection. "I remember as a child sitting and looking out my bedroom window at the trees and grass and hearing the music playing on my record player, and it gave me hope in the midst of despair, unpredictability, and tension in our home. This led to my singing," says Diane, "which has been the greatest joy of my life. I remember feeling part of something grand when we put on a musical program at church or school. With music, I was part of something that gave significance to my life."

The mother of my friend Mary died recently, and Mary shared how, in the midst of grieving, a whole stream of songs and hymns from childhood came to mind. As she sang them, tremendous comfort and assurance came to her, reminding her that God hasn't abandoned them, that heaven is a wonderful place her mother now lives in forever, and that good will come from even a difficult experience.

Music helps children clarify their feelings. You can talk about emotions in a song or instrumental piece—"Is this music sad or happy? What makes it seem that way?"

Music calls upon people to express their feelings more fully—singing, clapping, moving, dancing—individually or in a group. While often the understanding of music is intellectual only, it can also be perceived on physical and emotional levels.

BOOSTING SELF-ESTEEM

Music participation helps children feel a sense of worth and boosts their self-esteem. "John struggles in school," said his mother, Anna. "But what he loves is his music. He plans for months what he's going to do for the spring talent show. He writes special music for it and gets a group together to practice and perform his song. It is a wonderful way or him to express himself, and it's a real self-esteem builder. He's also building the momentum to tackle other challenges at high school."

"Music training has helped tremendously in my children's self-esteem," said Robin. "A lot of confidence develops in learning to do something well." As their performing skills develop from that first recital, getting up to play "Twinkle, Twinkle, Little Star" to later performances of Pachelbel's Canon in D, even shy children develop confidence as they learn to stand up in front of an audience, announce what they came to play, and do it!

MUSIC MAKING FOR SPECIAL EDUCATION AND LEARNING-DISABLED CHILDREN

Music participation is for all children, especially those with special needs. "My son is hearing-impaired, and his first special education teacher encouraged music lessons," says Diane. "Brad began flute lessons in fourth grade. They helped him develop perception of rhythm, tone, and pitch, and music competition was good for his self-esteem." The Ivymount School in Rockville, Maryland, helps children with developmental problems like mental retardation, autism, emotional disturbances, and severe to moderate learning disabilities. Ruthlee Adler, a music therapist at Ivymount, uses song and dance to help the children learn and cope.[7] She tells of one five-year-old boy who lacked fine motor skills and didn't know left from right. Through the boy's interest in the xylophone, Adler taught him his numbers and left from right. He eventually learned to read music, play the piano, and lead group singing.[8]

Sometimes we don't involve a special education child in music because of his disabilities. But as Connie Hoover, a Suzuki piano teacher says, "In my experience, there's not a child who cannot learn to play or sing, who can't overcome handicaps, if he is willing to work for it."

One of her students, Gary, had severe learning disabilities, attention deficit disorder with hyperactivity, and emotional and visual problems. He took lessons for eight years. He never learned to read music. "But it was amazing how beautifully he could play; his emotions came across," says Connie. "He mastered left hand–right hand coordination and intricacies, and he had a good ear for music, which really helped. Another major factor was the support of his mother during those eight years of lessons."

MUSIC IN THE FAMILY

From the earliest days of infancy, music is a significant part of the developing emotional connections between mother and child. And we know that early shared musical activities support and enrich the bonding between parent and child that can last a lifetime.

Music also offers many opportunities for shared family experiences like singing, playing instruments, listening to favorite recordings, attending concerts and recitals, and performing for and with family and friends. Music making enhances togetherness and cooperation, whether at school, church, or home.

Music can facilitate and enhance your relationship with your child even through adolescence. Author Al Menconi suggests that music can be a bridge of communication with your children, especially as they reach the preteen and teen years. You can share your values and help your child enjoy a favorite song of yours by opening your heart—and music—to your child. With music you also tune in to your child's thoughts and emotions.

Choose a song that expresses your own love for God, or how his grace enabled you to deal with a problem or loss in your life. Then here's what Menconi suggests:

> When you find an appropriate song, ask your kids for
> five minutes of their time. Explain that you would like to
> have them listen to a song that means a lot to you. Take
> one of your five minutes to give a little background and
> why you chose this song. Then have them read the lyrics
> with you while the song is played. Make sure they focus on
> the message of the song instead of its sound. Do your best
> to make this a pleasant experience, and don't force participa-
> tion if you haven't been communicating well up to this
> point.

The goal is to allow your family to share what you feel in your soul and to see your love for Jesus. Follow the song with a question or two.[9]

Menconi says that sharing your favorite songs with your child in this way can accomplish several things:

- Even if the song is not his or her favorite style, your child can begin to see Christian music as something "personal, deep, and interesting."
- You model vulnerability as you share your most important values and feelings with your child.
- It can lead to some interesting discussions about morals, spiritual issues, and values with your child.
- Children often begin to think of songs that speak personally to them and share them with you and others.
- Your child learns to evaluate his own music for "ministry value" and meaning, not just as entertainment.[10]

As we offer children quality music early in life and throughout their growing-up years, we are building a foundation of good taste, discernment, and an appetite for the best. They, in turn, will be better prepared to choose their own music when they are old enough to begin buying it.

Chapter Three

Portrait of a Musical Family

Music is…playing your own tune
while keeping time with the rest of the band.

UNKNOWN

Whether it's music study or raising children, sometimes parents find it helpful to get a big picture or a longer view of things. Let me share with you the journey of one family—the Nystroms of Saint Charles, Illinois—through the years of music making and lessons with their four children from the time they were babies through college and beyond.

Although Carolyn and Roger Nystrom were not musicians, they both loved music and wanted to pass that on to their children. Roger started learning to play a trumpet and drums in elementary school, but his music-playing stint was short-lived due to frequent moves. Carolyn longed to make music. But she grew up in a rural area with no funds for lessons or a piano. After a few months of working at her first job at age sixteen, she bought an old piano and paid for two years of lessons. When the church pianist left, she spent hours learning hymns and played for Sunday services during her senior year.

Carolyn and Roger wanted their children to have the opportunity to play musical instruments. At the Nystrom household, music was a constant for thirty years. When they had background music on, it was almost always the

Chicago classical station. After a while their kids knew the great works of music literature because they had always heard them.

As soon as the Nystrom children were able to sit in the highchair, Carolyn pulled it over to the piano and let them bang away. They loved it and soon made their own kinds of music. From those early days the children learned that music was something they could do and that the piano was not a forbidden piece of furniture.

When the children were between five and eight years old, their parents started them on piano lessons, being careful to select a teacher who was good with young children, excellent at teaching, and a fine pianist herself. Mom supervised practice, but rather loosely. Scheduled practice times, lots of encouragement, and occasional rewards spurred them on. "They had to practice a certain amount of time every day, but we didn't hang over them to see exactly what they did," says Carolyn.

When each of the children reached age nine, they started in the school stringed instrument program. Mom and Dad helped them select an instrument, rented a small one suited to their size, and signed them up for the free group lessons at school and for the school orchestras. Then there was more practicing to supervise! After they had been in the orchestra for about a year, they started private string lessons as well, again from qualified instructors. If the child made progress, when he or she was ready for a full-sized instrument at about age twelve to fourteen, they bought the best instrument they could afford.

The whole family attended all school music functions and concerts in the community—those for their own age and those for older kids, including a local college's music events—so that they could see where they were headed. Carolyn sat in on most of their lessons to observe how they were taught and to keep track of their progress. "I learned a lot of music myself that way," she says. And as soon as they could play appropriate music with confidence, their church invited each of the children to use their music in worship services.

"All of the kids got a little jaundiced about music lessons during the junior high years," says Carolyn. "But we insisted that they stick with it, even at a minimum level. By high school, they were excited about music again. I think they all would say they are glad we made them stay with it through that stage."

By high school, some of the Nystrom teenagers were taking as many as four lessons a week (voice, piano, stringed, and wind instrument). "By this time we were hoping they would cut down!" says Carolyn. And they did in fact begin to select what they most wanted to emphasize. Their younger son, Craig, dropped lessons altogether just prior to his high school junior year (but he started taking cello again in college). The other son, Randy, who is physically and mentally handicapped, stopped his viola lessons in mid-high school when his teacher died. But he still plays for fun when he wants to and occasionally talks about taking lessons again. The two girls continued to perform and study music through their college years.

"Supervised practice was not always a joy to any of us. And we always had the question of whether the child's objections were sufficiently strong to warrant dropping the lessons. To this day I'm not sure that we decided correctly," says Carolyn. They did find, however, that by age sixteen each child pretty much decreed what he or she would and wouldn't do. And the parents decided to live with it whether they liked it or not. In one case the older daughter, Sheri, insisted that her current violin teacher was not sufficient, even though he was less expensive than others, and that she would switch to a better and higher-priced teacher even if she had to pay for the lessons herself. She did. And she was right. Craig stopped practicing and taking his cello lessons at age sixteen, and that was that. He still remains a talented cellist, however. About that same age, Lori decided that playing flute was aggravating her TMJ (a problem in her jaw joint) just after they had purchased a full-priced silver flute. But she continued with cello, piano, and voice.

Sheri was the only one who made music her profession. And she loved it! She began teaching younger students (to earn money for her own lessons) when she was fourteen. By the time she graduated from high school, she had twenty students and was a very capable teacher. People in their community said she gave the best, nonthreatening, fun recitals they had ever attended. Young children loved her and so did their parents. Several years later the students she started on string instruments at age eight or nine were the backbone of the high school orchestra.

Sheri chose music education as her major in college. Even though she was a fine violist by that time, she turned her teaching interest toward the handicapped, having had plenty of practice in teaching her own handicapped brother, Randy. She wanted to teach students who would never be "good" at music to enjoy playing string instruments. As a music education major and an avid musician, she learned to play almost every instrument. She played viola in a string quartet. She played guitar for youth and camp ministry. She accompanied her students on piano. She played electric bass in a Christian rock band. Some of her parents' favorite memories are of the quartet and Sheri's other music groups, rehearsing in their living room. She even sang a duet with her husband at their wedding.

Two years later, at age twenty-two, Sheri and her unborn child died in a car accident, just weeks after she graduated from college. Her life was short, but it was full of the joy of music—and she filled her family's and friends' lives with it as well.

All of the Nystrom kids except Randy have used their music to earn money. String quartet players in their area, even high school students, can earn twenty dollars per hour. Lori sang in choir and played in an orchestra in college, and both groups went on extensive tours. While she does not continue to use her music professionally, she enjoys it tremendously, and her husband is a professional tenor in New York City.

Craig is now an adult. Even though he stopped his cello lessons for two years, he never stopped playing and earning money with his cello. And he loves all kinds of music.

Randy loves classical music. His favorite composers are Copland and Beethoven. Randy brought the whole audience to tears at his special-education school's Christmas program. He drew out his viola and played "Amazing Grace" in memory "of the best teacher I ever had, my sister."

Part Two

Musical Development
and Training

Chapter Four

Your Child's Musical Development

Music gives...wings to the mind, flight to the imagination,
a charm to sadness, gaiety and life to everything.

PLATO

Before you choose musical experiences for your child, it's important to have an understanding of the basic stages of musical development in children.

Sally Rogers, a child psychiatrist, says that "music appears to be a discrete area of learning, available for development and growth quite early in life, rather unrelated to other developmental accomplishments of young children (such as language, motor skills, social skills), but *quite dependent on environmental stimulation and training in order to develop fully.*"[1]

Every child has musical aptitude and potential. Shinichi Suzuki, master violin teacher, educational philosopher, and founder of the Suzuki Talent Education program, believed that each child is born with natural ability and tremendous potential. What makes the difference in whether the child's talent is developed, he felt, is a superior home environment and proper training.[2]

A report by Edwin Gordon, formerly professor of research in music education at Temple University in Philadelphia, showed that properly timed and sequenced early experiences with music can actually raise the child's musical aptitude.[3]

Creating a positive musical environment at home for your child between birth and age five is the most significant thing you can do to enhance his appreciation, aptitude, and ability in the area of music.

The descriptions of characteristics that follow do not comprise a definitive list, but offer a general framework as you plan experiences and goals for your child. As you reflect on these characteristics, keep in mind that children progress and develop at very different rates. Every child's brain development and musical development has its own timetable. In spite of this, we sometimes plan activities, commit to lessons, or convey expectations that are not appropriate for a child's developmental stage.

INFANTS: "TO BE BORN IS TO BE MUSICAL"

Newborns not only recognize their mother's voice, but differentiate between their mother's voice and other women's voices. Studies show that infants are sensitive to rhythm, intonation, and frequency variation.[4] In addition, they can discriminate between musical styles, even in the first days of life.[5]

Research also shows that even premature infants with many physical problems and limitations in development were immediately responsive to music. Premature babies responded to Beethoven's "Moonlight Sonata" with lower heart rate, lower blood pressure, and lower respiratory rate than they did to Khachaturian's "Sabre Dance."[6] Music also plays a significant part in the early bonding process between mother and child, as a mother sings lullabies to her infant while rocking and nursing her.

Studies and the experiences of mothers show that music also has a significant impact on the preborn infant. For example, Robin, mother of four children, noticed a big difference between the responses to opera of her oldest child, Annie, and her other three children. When Robin was pregnant with Annie, she was preparing for her senior vocal performance recital. Every day during most of the pregnancy (especially the last several months), Robin practiced singing opera.

In the first few months of Annie's infancy, her parents realized she was very responsive to opera. Annie would immediately stop crying if Robin sang to her. She would turn her little head to the side, closing her eyes as if listening intently. Songs from operas were some of her favorite music as a young child. In fact, Annie sang everything in an operatic style—"Joy to the World," "Jesus Loves Me," even "Old MacDonald Had a Farm"! She could match pitch and sing whole lines of songs even as a two-year-old.

Studies and experiences such as this suggest that "the musical mind, in body and spirit, is a natural birthright, an inherent part of our humanness."[7] And as a parent, you can do much to encourage your child's musical appreciation and development.

Surround babies with music. Sing to your baby while feeding, bathing, and riding in the car, using soft repetitive refrains like "Rock-A-Bye Baby," "Twinkle, Twinkle, Little Star," nursery songs, lullabies, and your own favorite melodies.

In this high-tech world, young mothers are often presented lullaby CDs at their baby showers. "When baby cries, the idea goes, they will be able to switch on the high-tech audio system and the little one will drift off—the voices of strangers in his ears," says Kathleen Cushman.[8] These and other recorded music collections are nice, but they can't replace a mother's voice soothing a feverish baby or singing a little one to sleep. Don't forget to give your child the gift of your own voice, the treasure of your own songs.

When your baby is fussy and needs calming, as you diaper and care for her and go about your day, sing favorite songs and sing about her. For example, say, "You look so sweet today! You are my little joy!" When you ride together in the car, sing happy songs, and she may enjoy sitting in her car seat a little more.

As your baby grows, read and sing nursery rhymes, play Pat-a-Cake, This Little Piggy, and lap games that connect words and melodies with gesture and movement (for example, "Ride a white horse to Banbury Cross..." while bouncing baby gently on your knee). When music is playing, clap baby's hands together and move them to the music.

Musical mobiles are wonderful to hang above the crib or cradle. Soft, stuffed animals that play a tune become favorite toys. By six to nine months, musical toys activated by knobs the baby can turn are fun. Play classical music, folk music, and favorite CDs from early days in the crib. Exposing children to beautiful music from an early age is important. When you play the same soothing classical music each night before bedtime, like a Mozart piano concerto, your baby associates that with sleep and relaxes more easily.

Play certain music right before dinner (and then repeat it daily) and marching or other cheerful music during your morning bathing-dressing-feeding routine to set the tone for the day.

Here's a wonderful musical idea for your baby: Make up a little song for your child that will be his or her "theme song." It's important that the song bless and affirm the child, incorporating whatever positive attributes the Lord shows you. Bill and Robin Wolaver wrote a song for each newborn built around the child's name, like this one for their fourth child, little Camille:

> Camille Rose
> Everybody knows
> Your name
> Camille Rose
> Never will there be another
> Quite the same
> Camille Rose
> Everybody knows your name
> And who can blame them?
> You're sweet as candy cane!

Just a carefree, fun song that's short and created around the name—they have sung this song often to baby Camille, from her earliest days, and find that it will quiet her when nothing else does. You could make a cassette tape, singing your baby's song and family favorites that you play before nap time and in the car.

Music is a wonderful soother and "cheerer-up," for little ones. Everybody needs some silence at certain times, so give your child the gift of quietness, too.

TODDLERS

Toddlers love to repeat and mimic. Some can imitate voice tones and pitch. But don't be alarmed if your toddler doesn't sing in tune yet. They can learn short simple tunes and love to listen to music and try to match body movement to simple musical beats. They rock, sway, move up and down, and enjoy clapping and action songs. Toddlers like to experiment with their voices. When playing, they often spontaneously sing or hum a favorite tune.[9] They enjoy listening to music tapes, especially when they can move or dance to the music.

I've found that the little two-year-olds I've taught in our "Merry Munchkin" Sunday school class learn and enjoy most when actively involving their hands, voices, and whole bodies. If we sing about our families, they love to have a mommy or sister or daddy doll to dance back and forth on the table. When I sing "the flowers are gently blowing, blowing in the wind," they each love to have a brightly colored silk flower they've picked from our "garden basket" to wave back and forth like the wind.

Toddlers enjoy exploring space by moving forward and backward, upward and downward, imitating the motions of others, and they show interest in rhythm instruments.[10]

This is a critical time for your child to have a rich and balanced diet of music experiences. These can include simple musical games and rhymes, singing and moving, dancing around the living room to music, creating a marching band parade, being sung to at bedtime, and simply listening to music. Toddlers especially enjoy musical push toys and stuffed animals. They also like listening to lively, joyful music like Raffi tapes[11] and collections of children's favorites, but they can enjoy classical music as well.

Some of the happiest, most memorable times you have with your toddler can be with music. Continue to sing to and with your toddler while doing chores, during play, before bedtime, and throughout the day. You can also make up your own songs together or make up new words for familiar tunes. When traveling or doing errands in the car, sing a song like "Old MacDonald Had a Farm," and let each person pick out an animal and make the sounds for the animals as you sing.

Near the age of three, children delight in singing along and acting out songs with hand or finger motions, so they begin to enjoy simple finger plays, like "Where Is Thumpkin?" "I'm a Little Teapot," and "This Old Man." Finger plays are good activities to fill a waiting or restless moment—at the doctor's office or waiting for Dad to come home.[12] Rhythm instruments like the tambourine, melody bells, or triangle can be used with children from toddler stage on through early elementary school. You can buy a set or make your own:

> *Maracas:* Put rice or beans in a plastic spice jar for an easy musical shaker.
>
> *Percussion instruments:* Pots and pans with a wooden spoon; or for a quieter one, make a drum out of an oatmeal box.
>
> *Rhythm sticks:* Two wooden dowel sticks from the lumberyard or hardware store, or use two pieces of thick garden cane.
>
> *Melody bells:* Sew bells on elastic for your child to wear on her wrists.

Rhythm instruments are the best way for a young child to learn to keep a steady beat and practice different rhythms—important foundations for later success on an instrument—while still having lots of fun. Your child can play the rhythm instrument and keep time to the music as you sing together or as a favorite recording plays. He can play loud, then play soft, then somewhere in between. Rhythm sticks tap the beat as your child marches or sings. Bells and tambourines are fun for dancing. A sense of rhythm will develop at different ages, so don't be alarmed if your child doesn't keep a steady beat yet. Make real instruments available also. Don't spank your toddler for playing the piano or bar him from touching it through his preschool years and then expect him to love taking piano lessons at age seven.

PRESCHOOLERS

The ability to imitate tunes continues to develop as children grow, and some preschoolers try to reproduce whole songs.[13] They may sing along on certain lines or phrases of familiar songs. Preschool children can usually keep a regular beat, and some can sing in tune. For others, the sense of musical pitch is undeveloped. Preschooler's voices tend to be small and have a limited range. Rhythmic response is most important, and creativity and spontaneity mark their music making.

Preschoolers enjoy listening to prerecorded music of many kinds and imitating motions. They are interested in rhythm instruments and have enough motor control to use them to follow along with the beat. Attention spans are relatively short, and preschoolers, like toddlers, enjoy music and movement for the sheer delight and fun it affords them, rather than for performance or skill development.[14]

Preschoolers seem to be in motion continually and are physically active, and their large-muscle control is more developed than their small muscles. Repetitive activity gives them a feeling of security.

A three- or four-year-old may pick out part of "Twinkle, Twinkle, Little Star" on the piano, but that doesn't mean it's time for formal lessons. Some four-year-olds may reproduce rhythmic patterns and understand concepts such as loud/soft and fast/slow. They can memorize more complicated finger plays or action songs like "Itsy Bitsy Spider" or "Hokey Pokey." Preschoolers are very aware of sounds and rhythms in the home and the world around them.

This is a good time to sing, clap, play rhythm instruments, and do a variety of body movements to different kinds of music. Preschoolers can also make up stories that describe the music they hear. There are some delightful group experiences for little children, such as Kodaly, Dalcroze Eurhythmics, and Orff, that introduce music in a fun way.[15] In group classes, children enjoy responding physically to melody, rhythm, and timing. They respond kinesthetically—with movement, with the whole body—to melody, high and low, rhythms, fast and slow, clapping the beat, marching, and engaging in singing games. These musical programs are developmentally appropriate for preschoolers.

While preschoolers need opportunities to sing, march, and drum on percussion instruments, they don't necessarily need formal instruction. If parents do start their child this early in Suzuki piano or violin lessons, they must be extremely creative and innovative to make practice interesting, exciting, and most of all, fun for their young child. This means the parent must be very involved in lessons and practice and refrain from putting on pressure for good performance, which usually produces burnout. Beginning lessons early takes lots of extra parental support. However, some experts, such as Dr. Jane Healy, say, "There is little reason to rush into skill-and-practice-oriented lessons before about age seven when the brain refines its ability to combine sequences from different senses."[16] Certainly, most children should wait until after reading instruction is well under way before learning to read music. (See chapter 5 on "Learning to Make Music.")

Steer away from preschool music programs and schools that emphasize the "product"—the performance—and thus tend to narrow and squelch creativity rather than enhance children's development. As one mom said, "My four-year-old went to music school two hours in the morning, two days a week, and after several months, Jay didn't want to go. When we talked about it, he said, 'I colored the grapes the wrong color. I didn't sing right.'" As the mother went and observed, she found that the children were supposed to sing loud, and if they did, they got M&M's. She realized this was indicative of their philosophy of music instruction: Do it loud and do it right! In addition, everything was aimed toward putting on a splashy performance in extravagant costumes for the parents. Many parents thought, *It's wonderful. The children look so cute on stage.* But the most important question to consider is, Are the music activities and experiences developmentally appropriate for the age group? *If music classes for preschoolers are performance oriented, they are probably for the adults instead of the children.* If you do choose a music preschool program or classes for your child, choose carefully and observe a class or two before your child is enrolled. And remember, many of the same music-making activities (singing, dancing, and movement) can be done at home without pressure or competition in a nurturing and loving environment.

Preschoolers love sing-along tapes and CDs in the car, and listening to quality music is therefore important. Since preschoolers do so much imitating, have them listen to singing that uses a full range, using the higher "head voice" as opposed to low, bass, throaty pop sounds. They will sing and internalize what they hear at this stage. Choose music that involves expressive elements like wonder and imagination. Children enjoy making their own marching band and marching around the room with brother, sister, or friend, using homemade or purchased rhythm instruments. Introduce games that involve singing and movement like "London Bridge" and "Ring a Ring of Roses."

At this age my children loved to sit on the floor as I played the guitar and we sang familiar choruses. They also liked to help strum the guitar while I chorded the strings. As Connie, a busy mother of three, observed, "Sometimes we play the piano and sing, but they quickly take over on the piano and kick me off the bench." Zachary (three and a half) and Kathryn (two) play a piano duet they devised called "The Storm." Zachary plays the "thunder" and Kathryn plays the "rain." Kathryn also enjoys putting on one of her "dancing dresses" and twirling to the music. Connie takes her preschoolers to the philharmonic family concerts and special children's concerts, introduces them to musicians, and discusses the sounds of different instruments. They listen to many types of music.

At this age children love to be with their parents. Sharing music gives the child and parent quality time together. Studies show that the emotional environment created in and through musical interactions is most important in musical development. Parents who value music demonstrate to their children the importance of music and its role in their lives. Researchers who studied the effects of early music experiences on children said, "Our own guess is that the parent's own singing was probably the most important variable in the musical development of children."[17]

Make a game out of pitch matching with your children. You can sing, "What do you want for breakfast?" and they can mimic the melody as they answer, "Oh, I think I'll have eggs this morning!" Try a game in which you clap a rhythm pattern and the children repeat it exactly as they hear it. Dancing spontaneously to music, listening to classics, folk songs, Scripture set to music, singing together as a family—all enhance a child's musical development and appreciation.

KINDERGARTEN AND FIRST GRADE

Five- and six-year-olds may sing complete songs from memory and attempt to pick out tunes on musical instruments. They often show real interest in the piano and may put their fingers on the piano keys and experiment with "chords" but are not necessarily ready for formal lessons. Handedness becomes established, and large and small motor skills are developing. They want very much to be liked and to please their parents, so joining parents and teachers in musical activities is a big thrill.

Six-year-olds (and some fives) can sing in tune. They respond to a steady beat and enjoy marching to music, skipping to music, or playing active games with singing. However, even at age six, hand-eye coordination is not always synchronized.

Cooperation is a hallmark of kindergartners and first graders. At this stage the child enjoys singing with a group, taking turns, and playing musical games in which words are repeated over and over.

They may create songs on instruments and like to improvise. They can learn simple dance steps and combine creative drama with movement and singing. Five- and six-year-olds are developing a longer attention span for listening to recorded music. They enjoy cooperative playing and musical activities in small groups or with a partner.[18]

The most important factor is *enjoying* music together. Five- and six-year-olds have fun singing in the car, making up new verses to songs, and making silly sounds to a song instead of singing words. This is a wonderful time to take children to some concerts. Check with universities and colleges in your area to see if they have children's or family series of orchestra concerts, ensemble recitals, or musical theater. One mom said, "We took our son to hear a children's folk singer he had a tape of, and then bought the songbook to take home—a double reinforcement!" If your child is taking violin and you hear of a violinist playing a concert, take him and make it a special occasion.

When children are this age, it is important that they hear a lot of music, as well as see a love for music modeled in parents. Sing around the house, play CDs, enjoy your own music. When kids see that music is important to parents, they enjoy it even more.

Help your child become an active listener. When your child listens to classical or other music, ask her, "What kind of instrument is that? I hear a flute and a violin. What do you hear? How does it make you feel—happy or sad?"

Although Bill and Robin Wolaver's children all take piano, violin, or cello instruction and have plenty of practice, there are times they are goofy with music too. While the children play Bach on the cello, Dad accompanies them

on the piano in a country and Western, Japanese, or jazz style. It adds a measure of enjoyment to lighten up sometimes and not be too serious.

Since children love to create sounds, you might provide an instrument at
home such as a recorder, lap autoharp, or ukulele. (These instruments usually
come with an easy how-to-play book.)

Buy your child his own cassette tapes and an audiocassette player he can
operate himself. (See appendix B for suggestions on a variety of music.) When
singing together, ask, "Can you sing louder? softer? jerkier? smoother?"

Games like Follow the Leader, Swinging Statues (directions follow), and
rhythmic jingles for jumping rope are favorites of children and provide them
opportunities for practice and improvement of listening skills and muscular
control.

> *Follow the Leader:* The leader chooses a song to sing and
> decides how he will move to the music—hopping, swaying,
> doing high kicks, or slithering along. Everybody sings and fol-
> lows his movement. Or the leader can pick a recorded song
> and everyone follows him as he marches, skips, jumps, or
> moves to the music.

> *Swinging Statues:* Music plays, and everyone moves around the
> room in whatever way he wants. When the music abruptly
> stops, each child "freezes" into a statue. When the music starts,
> the children move again, and the game continues. This was
> one of my favorites as a child.

> *Jumping Rope:* You can find books in the library listing
> hundreds of jump rope games. This one involves chanting,
> singing, rhythm, and timing (and is great exercise) to a rhyme
> like "Mother, Mother":

>> Mother, Mother, I am sick
>> Call for the doctor, quick, quick, quick!
>> In came the doctor; in came the nurse.
>> In came the lady with the alligator purse.
>> Out went the doctor; out went the nurse;
>> Out went the lady with the alligator purse.

Also at mealtimes, you can sing the dinner prayer or blessing sometimes
instead of just saying it.

ELEMENTARY SCHOOL YEARS

At age seven, children will repeat and practice something over and over in order to master a skill. Sometimes they set goals that are too high for themselves and want to be perfect, causing frustration,[19] so they need a lot of encouragement. However, if you have laid the groundwork in your child's life thus far with singing, listening, and lots of participation in music, you'll really get to enjoy seeing the result as your child's musical skills blossom.

Children ages seven to nine begin to crave competency, mastery, and rules. They concentrate better on lessons and skill practice and thus benefit from formal music lessons. By eight years old, many children increase in speed and smoothness in their fine motor performance and muscular dexterity, have developed good reading skills, and can work independently. And by nine, two hands can be used independently and the fingers show new differentiation. Hand-eye coordination improves as attention span increases. A child at this age likes to display his skills and has better control over the sounds he produces. He enjoys the accomplishment of performing on musical instruments.[20] And he can sing from memory a whole repertoire of songs learned at school or in church choir.

This is an important time for high-quality models of creative expression in music, art, and dance, as well as enrichment experiences at home, school, and in the community. Going to concerts, ballets, and musical theater performances can enrich your child's life and provide good role models.

Children thrive on encouragement and acceptance from parents, teachers, and classmates as they cooperate and make music in groups. Since group activities are appealing at this age, valuable experiences may include playing in an Orff ensemble at school, singing in the children's choir at church, learning to play an instrument either through private or school lessons, and being part of the orchestra or band.

In the elementary years, children can enjoy listening to many types of music. Continue playing music daily in your home, perhaps tuning in to a radio station that includes many types of music, such as classical, folk, and international styles. Help your child start his own tape or CD collection of his all-time favorites, and add to it at birthday or Christmastime.

Elementary-age children vary greatly in their singing ability. Some sing very melodiously, and some are still unable to sing in tune at ages seven and eight. However, by ages nine to eleven the singing voice gradually improves in quality and range as the vocal cords and lungs develop. A sense of harmony begins to develop. If a child is not singing in tune at this age, it could be that he only needs a little encouragement or instruction in pitch-matching.

A mistake parents often make at this stage is to assume that a child has no musical ability if he or she sings off-key (and often boys up to age eight or ten sing in a monotone). This is not necessarily so. It may mean that the child hasn't been exposed to good singing, hasn't had experiences to develop this skill, or is just late in developing pitch.

Singing along with the child is one of the best ways to help. Sing with your child and help him move his voice up and down. Do some pitch-matching exercises: Say, "Listen to the tone as I sing your name, and then make the sound… Your name is Robby!" When you're singing, ask, "Can you make your voice move up?" Demonstrate with two or three notes, and then have him imitate the sounds and move his voice up. You are helping him realize that his voice is like an instrument and he can move it up and down. If your child has trouble singing on pitch, get close to his ear and softly sing in a nice range. Remove distractions to help him really hear what you're singing and lock in to the sound. After listening, he can then sing the same tones.

You can also make music part of your family's holiday traditions. Play Christmas recordings as you decorate the tree and throughout the Advent season. On Christmas Eve let each family member hold a lighted candle and sing "Silent Night," "Away in a Manger," "Joy to the World," and other carols. Invite friends and have an annual caroling party, or go as a family to carol at a nursing home or at homes of shut-ins. At Christmas my friends the Hooks invite another family over (and their instruments). Everyone plays and sings Christmas carols and enjoys cookies afterward.

This is a good age to get to know the great composers (see chapter 10). On each composer's birthday, you can read his biography, check out recordings of his music from the library, and celebrate his birthday.

Let your child get to know a musician! My friends Penny and Richard have invited musicians from the local city orchestra to be their guests at dinner or to stay overnight if lodging was needed for a special performance. As a family they attended the concert, and then their children got to visit with the musician in their home afterward.

If you have a computer at home, a software program that allows your child to write and perform original music is a great resource. With one program, Songwriter, the child can experiment with time and melody to create single-voice compositions. With others, they can print out the score of a song on the computer. In the first grade, Annie Wolaver (with a little help from Dad) wrote a new verse for "Twinkle, Twinkle, Little Star," entered it on the computer, and printed it out noted on manuscript paper.

During middle and later elementary years, depending on the children's level of playing, they can use their music skills to perform—to bring comfort, joy, and entertainment to others—like my friend Kyser, who at age nine played and sang for elderly residents at a local nursing home, and Annie, who at nine was a strolling violinist at a Laura Ashley dress shop during the Christmas season.

Neighborhood Music Festival and Karaoke Tapes

Plan an impromptu music festival and let your kids invite their friends to the fun. Karaoke tapes are a great chance for kids to try out their talents. A karaoke tape is a recorded musical accompaniment that the child can sing along with and feel like a recording artist. If your child has a portable microphone that attaches to her tape recorder, it's even better.

Karaoke tapes are found at many music and media stores and Christian bookstores, and offer many styles of music: contemporary Christian songs, hymns, children's songs, songs from musicals and movies like *Beauty and the Beast* or *Aladdin,* and "oldies but goodies." Each cassette contains the song with lyrics on one side and the musical accompaniment on the other side; printed words to the song are also included. After selecting the karaoke tape each child wants to perform with, provide some practice time so they can learn when to come in and when to wait for the instrumental parts. Practicing is a big part of the fun, and duets or trios may evolve in addition to solos. Karaoke practice sessions can take place in the car while you're doing errands, or after school with friends over. It's a great way for kids, even shy children, to stretch their talents. In addition to singing with karaoke tapes, children can plan to sing a song (or play a favorite recorded song) and accompany themselves with rhythm instruments—store-bought or homemade (see instructions for homemade rhythm instruments in the section "Toddlers"). Any child who plays an instrument—piano, guitar, trumpet, violin—can perform a solo number. Play a few music games, serve refreshments, and a wonderful time will be had by all!

Chapter Five

Learning to Make Music

Musical training is a more potent instrument than any other;
because rhythm and harmony find their way
into the inward places of the soul.

PLATO

My son is five and musically inclined," said one mom. "How can I encourage his musical talent and interest without pressuring him into lessons too early?"

"My daughter has been taking piano for two years, and now says she hates it!" said another mother at a recent parent meeting. "She wants to quit. Should I force her to continue or let her stop?"

Questions like these are asked at almost every parent group I speak to. How can we support our child in music study so that he or she stays interested and motivated? How do we deal with the second mom's dilemma, what I've come to call "piano slump," when our child loses interest? Are music lessons for all children, and at what age should they start? Let's look at these questions and some of the positive ways we can support our child in music study and enjoyment.

BENEFITS OF MUSIC STUDY

Learning to play an instrument, like developing any skill, can be a real self-esteem builder for children. And lessons can be lots of fun! Besides the enjoyment, the study and practice of music enhances creativity, social skills, cognitive abilities, coordination, concentration, and memory skills. The music student who sticks with practice on a regular basis becomes a more disciplined person and learns to stay calm under pressure. "There's nothing like the joy of learning something that looks so difficult, almost impossible at first," says one veteran student, "but it's amazing what we can make our fingers do!" Overcoming hurdles and completing a task like a composition that is entirely learned and even memorized gives a great sense of accomplishment. Music is a wonderful avenue of self-expression; you play a piece with your own personal interpretation—it is creative development within a structure.

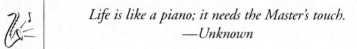

Life is like a piano; it needs the Master's touch.
—Unknown

Group lessons and experiences promote cooperation and teamwork, problem solving, and fellowship, and provide a good opportunity for socialization and interaction among the different children participating and the teacher. Music lessons also teach kids to cope with people outside their family. Sometimes children ages three to eight enjoy group lessons more than private instruction because they perceive less pressure. The teacher is looking at and working with the whole group, not just singling out one child, and they enjoy the social aspects of a group experience. Kids eight and older can benefit from the individual attention of private lessons; some younger children get distracted in groups and do better in private lessons or are at a level of proficiency at which individual study is best.

To Take or Not to Take?

When (and if) music lessons are started depends on the individual child and the family. While preschoolers and kindergartners need frequent, ongoing chances to sing, march, and drum on percussion instruments, some teachers feel that they don't need to have formal instruction or learn to read music.

Preschool enrichment classes, such as Kodály, Dalcroze Eurhythmics, KinderMusic, and Orff, are not only fun for kids, but lay a foundation for developing music skills. These methods often accelerate later progress on an instrument. (See appendix A for further information on methods of preschool music instruction.) Preschoolers usually thrive in enrichment programs where there is singing, dancing, and the general enjoyment of music. Loosely structured or low-key classes are best, in which the teacher focuses on the activity (such as responding physically with rhythm instruments to melody, rhythm, and timing) rather than the end result.

There are many different opinions on the best age for beginning skill-and-practice-oriented music instruction; in the final analysis, it depends on the child and his developmental level, the parents, and the approach of the teacher. Suzuki teachers feel that children can start lessons at ages two to four. Connie Hoover, a Suzuki teacher for thirteen years, says the process of "listen, absorb, and do it" is like the process of learning to talk. Children hear us speak and do it. In a similar way, she says, they learn to play by ear and listen repeatedly to tapes of pieces before they learn them. She starts her students at age three. (Her own daughters began Suzuki violin lessons at the age of two.) A key element in this method of early music instruction is that a parent is involved in all lessons and practices. Later children learn to read music, but usually after they learn to read in school.

On the other hand, some experts feel that beginning formal lessons at ages seven or eight, after the child has developed basic reading skills, is best. Marilyn Rosfeld, who holds a Ph.D. in piano performance and pedagogy and has taught privately and at the college level for over twenty years, says it's best to start lessons about the middle of the second grade or the beginning of third grade, when the child can read and motor coordination is better. In the years prior to lessons, it's important to build a solid foundation that combines listening, singing, participating, and enjoying music.

Some children are ready earlier than others, and some benefit by waiting. Your child's interest in music, an attention span that is up to half an hour's concentration or more, physical and hand-eye coordination that are developed to an appropriate level for handling an instrument, and the child's eagerness to learn are all signs of readiness.

"Progress is slower when they're younger. You might pay for two years of lessons for what can be accomplished in six months if the child is 'ready,'" says Rosfeld. "Teaching a child to hear, enjoy, and respond to music is the best thing for the preschooler."

(See chapter 4, "Your Child's Musical Development," on ways to stimulate and encourage the child's musical ability at each developmental level.)

The Talent Issue: Are Music Lessons for Every Child?

Sometimes we feel that music lessons are only for children who are "talented." Let me share with you a mistake we made in regard to our oldest son. During his elementary years, Justin was in a small Christian school that had no music training or orchestra opportunities at all, so we would have had to find a private teacher if he was to have lessons. He had a little bit of trouble staying on pitch when he sang, in contrast to his younger brother and sister, who seemed to have perfect pitch and more aptitude. They began piano lessons in first and third grades. But although we involved Justin in tennis and other pursuits, we didn't encourage him musically or arrange music lessons.

As Justin became a teenager, we realized he loved music, perhaps more than anyone else in our family. Now as an adult he still loves music, but one of his greatest regrets is that he didn't have a chance to learn to play an instrument when he was younger. As it turns out, he has a really nice voice. We goofed!

Every person has some musical aptitude, the capacity to respond to musical sound and to control the body's movement in order to create music. It is easier for some children to learn to play a musical instrument than others, due to different levels of dexterity or hand-eye coordination. Some sing in tune and stay on pitch early, and some are late bloomers. Although music aptitude varies among children, what we call talent seems to have more to do with achievement, discipline, and practice, how rich the home environment is musically, and the family's commitment to progress in music study. Suzuki believed that all children have ability and that their potential is absolutely unlimited—but that ability must be nurtured.

"All children have musical ability, but like IQ, not everybody is born with the same music IQ," says John Feierabend. "Whatever the child's music IQ at birth, it will atrophy if not stimulated. Even if a child has a high music aptitude, if not stimulated and nurtured, abilities will decline and by six to eight years old, this child will be less musical than other children." And the child born with a low music intelligence especially deserves to be in a rich musical environment, so that he won't lose what potential he has and can develop true enjoyment of music throughout his life.

Some children from a very early age show signs of what researchers like Dr. Howard Gardner of Harvard University call "musical intelligence" or a high music IQ. This is the child who loves sounds early on. In a sense, you could say he has a fine-tuned recorder in his brain that is extrasensitive to music. Even as a little child he can remember a song after hearing it only once. He learns new melodies quickly and can imitate tone and rhythm. The musically intelligent child often sings well from an early age, has "perfect pitch," and can pick out songs by ear on instruments. Interestingly, usually these children come from homes where they are surrounded by music and a parent or sibling plays instruments. This kind of special musical aptitude may be needed if one is going to make a career in music, but it is not a necessary ingredient for being successful at piano or other instruments.

Making music is not only for the few gifted people or those who do it with ease. Playing an instrument is a skill that can be learned, developed, practiced, and polished. And every child has great potential to enjoy and make music for a lifetime.

SELECTING A TEACHER

It is important to choose the best possible music teacher for your child. The rapport is critical between teacher and student, and not all good performers make good teachers. Good instruction requires genuine concern about the child and what his or her capabilities are. Is the teacher enthusiastic, and does she show a love for music? Lessons should be encouraging, not discouraging, and much of how positive or negative the experience is depends on the teacher.

Finding a teacher who fits and connects with your child will greatly enhance music study. We found this out by trial and error! One year when we were looking for a piano teacher for Alison, a mom I knew recommended her daughter's piano teacher. They liked her, so I just made the arrangements by phone, and we arrived at her house and started lesson one. Before long, piano lessons became the dreaded time of the week. Alison was making little progress and was not enjoying her music because she was afraid of making mistakes.

Although the teacher was proficient, she was high-strung, an extreme perfectionist, and somewhat critical. For Alison, being a sensitive child who worked best in an encouraging, warm atmosphere, this was not a good fit.

It is in learning music that many youthful hearts learn to love.—Ricard

We learned that it's best to get together first—parent, child, and prospective teacher—and talk about each person's expectations and the teacher's style of teaching. Ask to audit a lesson and perhaps hear other students in a recital. Does the teacher make lessons interesting? Would her approach spark your child's desire to learn music? Observe as the teacher works with your child during an introductory session on the piano or instrument. How do they interact?

You might ask about the teacher's educational background, about what kind of materials she uses, the policies of her studio, and her goals for accomplishment. Ask whether the teacher is a member of a professional musical organization—such as the Music Teachers National Association, the Music Educators National Conference, or the National Guild of Piano Teachers—each of which have specific competitions and workshops your child would participate in at local and state levels. These organizations also have continuing education opportunities whereby teachers update their own skills, become familiar with new literature, and learn new techniques.

You are looking for a teacher who will develop a warm personal relationship with your child, make lessons fun and motivating, help him learn to enjoy music more, and affirm his progress.

HELPING YOUR CHILD SUCCEED AT MUSIC LESSONS

Here are some ways to get off to the best possible start when music lessons begin:

Go into music lessons with the attitude that, as parent and child, you are entering a commitment together. You're committing to the following: a certain time frame; that lessons and practice will be a family priority; and that it's going to be enjoyable some of the time and not at other times. "If the child takes only two years and stops lessons, it's money down the drain," says Marilyn Rosfeld, "because she won't have the skills that last. With four or five years of lessons and average practice, you have established the basics and learned enough to pick up music again in college or later."

Establish goals. "You have to give kids goals," advises piano teacher Dianne Phillips. "And sometimes we have to bribe them! We all work for rewards; we want an A in a class or a job and a salary. Even though we want to get them to play for the intrinsic reasons, it starts with extrinsic motivations, like stars or stickers for playing a song five times in a row. A parent might say, 'If you're consistent with practice for three weeks we'll go to the *Peter and the Wolf* concert and out for ice cream,' or 'When you finish learning this piece, we'll make a video for Grandma and Grandpa.' It's also valuable to do ensembles with other young musicians. Music contests and awards are motivational. Children want a good score, but they also benefit by seeing other kids who take music lessons."

Be aware of the teacher's goals for your child (for example, finishing Books

1 and 2 by recital, or memorizing five pieces of music) so that you can support and encourage those goals. You can also help your child readjust goals if they are not realistic or are causing too much pressure.

Be involved in your child's practice. Parental involvement in music study is one of the most motivating factors.

"When both our children first began music lessons (flute, piano, and clarinet), I sat with them through each practice session for the first few years," said Phillips. "I really feel this was very important in getting them off to a good start."

"Lessons are a high priority in our life as a family—practicing and being prepared, meeting definite goals—and the most significant thing that's encouraged their music is our participation," said Robin, mother of four, three of whom take Suzuki violin and cello lessons. Part of the success of the Suzuki program is that when the child takes classes, the parent is also enrolled; the burden of learning is not all on the child's shoulders.

Robin has also found that if she and the older child in a family are involved together in practice lessons, the younger children want this kind of one-on-one time too. Their three-year-old has a pretend violin and asks, "Mama, is it my time to practice?" This direct parental role in practice may diminish as a child gets older and becomes more self-reliant and proficient on the instrument. But the older child or teenager doesn't outgrow the need for a parent's sincere interest and enthusiasm; even then they want Mom or Dad to sit in the room from time to time while they practice and enjoy hearing them play.

Although mothers are usually more involved than fathers, research shows that a dad's positive response and interest can be a very significant influence on children's progress. I know my father's enthusiasm about our music lessons and his asking us to play for him at home was the big motivator to practice. When a dad attends his child's recitals, listens to an occasional practice, and shows he is pleased, it offers a real boost! It doesn't matter if he can sing or play an instrument himself; it's Dad saying, "Play for me," and offering encouragement that counts. If the father is absent, grandparents can assume this role and offer encouraging support.

Establish a daily practice routine. Your child's teacher can recommend the amount of daily practice expected. For homeschooled children, morning practice before school or other activities works well. For others, practice after school and before dinner may work. Two short daily practice times may work better than one longer practice period, especially if the student is younger or tired or hasn't developed a long attention span. Find whatever practice routine is best for your child's age, needs, and schedule (which change as he or she grows), but aim for consistency (perhaps posting a schedule on the refrigerator), and make your child's practice a family priority. Have good lighting, privacy (without the television on next to the piano), and a well-tuned piano for the practice sessions.

Be aware of the differences in children's temperaments and work with instead of against them. For example, some kids are natural organizers; they like to make a list of things to do each day and follow it. These children thrive on setting goals for their music or making a chart and using stars to keep track of practice sessions.

Some kids are motivated more by praise and by getting a vision of how much fun it will be to perform. Say things like "Your teacher is going to be so pleased at all the effort you've put into this piece!" or "We're going to enjoy your music so much at the recital." This child, who tends to be spontaneous and fun, needs to practice in palatable chunks and have lots of encouragement.

Make opportunities to play the instrument and share music experiences regularly within the family. For Angela, a fourteen-year-old, her family's incorporating music into their everyday lives has made all the difference. "Dad sings all the time, plays the trumpet, guitar, and recorders. He improvises music into all kinds of things. Sometimes he plays his trumpet or guitar while I accompany him on the piano. Mother plays the piano and sings. They have taken me to the inner-city mission and to nursing homes and given me a chance to sing or play for the people. I've also played at church. We've had fun times with music and hear good music on the stereo. Sometimes I get tired of practice and they tell me they are spending a lot on lessons (guilt!) or that they'll find a teacher who is harder. But I went to visit my aunt and uncle for two weeks and nearly went crazy because they didn't have a piano. I realized then how much the piano means to me!"

In the Hook family, when Leslie, age nine, gets to play her violin and John, age six, plays his cello along with Dad's cello or guitar, it's a wonderful time of togetherness and fun.

For preschoolers, having an audience at home is a great motivation booster. One family has a "Show-and-Tell Night" every week, where each member of the family has three minutes to perform or share whatever they want—sing a song, play a new piece on their instrument, read poetry, or even demonstrate new karate moves! Dad may do a dramatic reading of a Bible story. One night the children may put on a play they have created. A child may tell stories he makes up. Another child may play her violin. It is their children's absolute favorite time of the week, and they look forward to it and prepare. The response of the rest of the family to each person's contribution? Total acceptance and applause—no criticism. It gives them an opportunity to explore different ways of being creative and to practice performing in front of an audience.

If Benjamin is working on trying to hold his bow correctly on his cello, his mother says, "We're going to perform this for Dad on Thursday." And then Dad makes a point to affirm and praise Benjamin's effort at clean bowing. This is a special thing, done only a couple of times a month, but it motivates him in something that might otherwise be tedious work.

Make recital day special! "I'll never forget our recital days when I was growing up," says Robin. "We got to stay home from school [not that I'm suggesting that!], take a nap, get new shoes and formal dresses, and afterward we all went out to eat as a family. My parents were missionaries and we didn't have a lot of money; oh, how we loved the special dinner afterward! Those days are so vivid in my memory. When parents make recital times a big deal, it shows their children how they value their music."

Stay in touch with the teacher and student about the music. "For the student to know that her parent cares and appreciates what she does is the most important thing," says one teacher. Not every week, but periodically, check in to see what the teacher is aiming for and what the student is doing and trying to do.

You can show interest by listening to your child practice and talking with him about the lessons and practice, asking, "How did it go? Let me hear your favorite piece that you're working on."

"Don't force lessons; instead encourage," says Anna, mother of two very musical teenagers. "They're the ones who have to be committed to practicing, and music is a heart thing, not a mechanical thing."

Get your child involved in some music group—a band, small ensemble, or youth orchestra, especially during the adolescent years. Small groups at church and school help young people feel that they belong.

NUDGING YOUR CHILD OUT OF PIANO (OR OTHER INSTRUMENT!) SLUMP

When Angie was a preschooler she often sat at the piano, picking out tunes and playing her own little melodies. So her parents put her in piano lessons. Angie took them for a year, lost interest, and wanted to quit. What can her parents do?

Or what should you do and say if your child decides after a few weeks or months of lessons, "I'm no good at this at all! I don't want to take lessons anymore!"

If a "slump" does occur, here are some ways to rekindle the motivation and enjoyment of playing:

Have a change of music. Sometimes a change out of a book the student has been in for months to a piece of sheet music or a contemporary piece helps. "I find many students who haven't made any progress in six months learn five or six Christmas songs in two weeks!" says Marilyn Rosfeld. Let the teacher know about your child's waning interest, and ask that she introduce a piece that is fun. Switching to new music can be a real motivator.

Be supportive and cooperative about practice at home. Often teachers find that the parent is undermining the child's motivation without realizing it. Heather starts to practice, and Dad says, "Can't you practice later? The news is on." Nicholas begins practicing his scales, and Mom says, "Can you stop practicing now? My favorite show is coming on." If this is the problem, limit your television watching or move the piano to another place in the house where your child can practice freely.

Give encouraging words instead of criticism. One day a mom said to her son's piano teacher (with him standing there), "I can't believe Brian is still playing this piece after nine months and it still sounds just terrible." Instead of criticizing, or saying, "Not that again!" when your child starts to practice a piece, offer compliments regularly. Think of positive, encouraging words to say to your child about his playing and practice. Overpraising is not necessary, but children need sincere encouragement and appreciation for their efforts, perseverance, and specific skills they've worked hard on.

Encourage your child to have fun with his instrument. To be creative, pick out a favorite song by ear, improvise, compose, and experiment with new sounds.

Give children reasons to play and share their music. This will help them avoid "piano slump" or deal with it when it comes. Having an opportunity to perform and use their music is a real motivator— accompanying sister on the flute for a family reunion, playing a duet with someone in which the child plays the easier part for a talent show, or participating in informal recitals.

"One of the best things school and church music directors can do is to ask children to accompany the choir on a piece and give them opportunities to use their music at church. Send around a list to keep track of who plays what instrument, and for how long, so that you know who is likely to be ready for this kind of task," says Rosfeld. Every spring she holds a Sunday afternoon recital when any child or teenager in the church who plays an instrument or sings can perform and share his or her talents.

When students still want to quit, what can parents do? Here's what one teacher said: "Parents are too soft. They let kids make the decision to quit, when it's impossible for children to know the long-term value of continuing lessons. If the lessons have been committed to, they should be considered a necessary part of the student's education. Just as they are not in a position to decide if they should quit math if they don't like learning long division, it shouldn't be the child who makes the decision to quit."

Another said, "I hear so many adults who quit lessons as children express regrets: 'I wish my parents hadn't let me quit.' But I've never heard an adult who regretted continuing his or her music lessons."

"Piano slump is a communication problem," says Dianne Phillips, a piano teacher for more than twenty-five years. "Parents need to be aware that, when children reach a plateau, their fingers have to catch up with what their brains have learned, and they often get frustrated and into a slump because they think they aren't progressing. But we need to practice the skill to master it (just as adding and subtracting are fun at first, then old hat, but they must be continued before multiplication and division can be learned). The fingers must practice a piece over and over until it becomes the natural thing to do. If parents expect that getting discouraged is normal during the plateau, that learning comes in spurts, and that there will be a new spurt of learning after the plateau, then they can encourage their child."

> *Music is…a demanding enterprise;*
> *you must do it with love or not at all.*—*John Bowles*

When Melissa becomes discouraged or frustrated over some difficult piece, her parents' praise and encouragement seem to be the most important factors in helping her keep on with lessons and practice. "We remind her of past accomplishments, and she is challenged to work hard," says her mother. "She truly loves music, especially piano, and that in itself keeps her motivated."

"Our son doesn't have quite the motivation and organization his older sister has, but we've agreed that we'll never let him quit during a slump," said another parent. If a child has a special hurdle to get over, she gets all the more discouraged during the difficult times when she's not as excited about playing the instrument. But if you can see her through that low point (offer a change in music, change in practice time, make an effort together to get through the slump), then after the recital and accomplishment, sit down and discuss the issue of taking lessons: Is this the direction you want to continue to take?

Finally, look at the long term and help your child see it too! Once a young person has a solid musical foundation on the piano, he can easily branch out to a different instrument. Things learned while playing the keyboard transfer to other instruments—notation, rhythm, meter, dynamics—and that's why a large number of kids who play piano become proficient at other instruments.

John, for example, took piano for eight years, then played percussion instruments and horn, and now can play almost any instrument.

While your child is taking music lessons, expose him to a wide variety of music, including concerts in the community and recitals—especially when there is a concert or performance that features an artist playing your child's instrument. Not only does a background of good music create a peaceful, uplifting atmosphere, but it makes music a natural part of a student's worldview so that the classical works, like Mozart's, don't sound foreign or inaccessible. If your child is surrounded by music, he will develop some ownership of it, will not be so easily intimidated by it, and will look forward to mastering it for himself.

Remember, a child's musical life should not be full of pressure. Her schedule shouldn't fill up totally with classes. If you book every minute of your child's after-school time, she'll eventually burn out or rebel. There needs to be time to play outside, read, make a tent in the backyard or living room, be with friends, and even do nothing.

"There is plenty of time to prepare for a musical career if that becomes a goal," said Frank Wilson, M.D., codirector of the 1987 Music and Child Development Conference and professor of neurology at University of California School of Medicine. "Just as there are many of us who enjoy jogging for fun and have no intention of competing in the Olympics, your child should be encouraged to experience what music affords, based on his or her own instincts and interests."

HOW CAN CHILDREN LEARN TO PLAY MUSICAL INSTRUMENTS WITHOUT FORMAL LESSONS?

Sometimes formal music lessons are not an option for our children because of finances, location, or scheduling. In that case, how can children learn to play instruments without a teacher? Learning to play an instrument without a private instructor is not as difficult as it sounds. In fact, with the technology of computers and videos, and the variety of musical products, it can be an enjoyable adventure. For example, there is "The Miracle Piano," an electronic keyboard that connects to your computer. With it your child is guided by a piano teacher on screen and can progress at his own pace. Whether it's a guitar or recorder your child wants to learn, all you need are your child's enthusiasm and yours, the instrument, an instructional guide book and aids—and you'll be on your way to music-making fun. Here are some instruments and suggestions.

Recorder. Usually quite inexpensive and made from wood or high-quality molded plastic, this instrument is easy to learn to play. The recorder is simple but has a two-octave range with all the notes in-between; this makes recorder study a means of learning to read music. There are different sizes of recorders: soprano (smallest and good size for a young child starting out), alto (little larger), and bass (longest recorder, lowest sound).

The instructional books show where to put your fingers to play notes, how to hold the recorder, and other tips on how to change notes quickly and smoothly and what to do if the notes you are playing sound squeaky or wobbly. There are many good recorder books to choose from.

Also check your local music store, children's toy store, learning shop, and catalogs for how-to videos or packaged recorder starter sets. In such sets, you get a soprano recorder, an instruction book, and play-along CDs—everything a student needs to get started. Even if you have little music experience, you can work with your child to learn the basics. He will be much more motivated with someone else participating. That's why your involvement or that of a sibling or friend is important.

A child of six or seven usually has the finger coordination and motor skills to be successful on the recorder. If your child is under age nine or ten, you would need to interpret the book and give guidance. Perhaps you could buy an alto recorder; your child could play soprano, and you could learn together and play duets.

If you know several other children who are interested, get a small recorder group together and find an adult (college student, school music teacher, etc.) to work with them. You could also request recorder group lessons at a community center or YMCA program.

Guitar. This is one of the most popular instruments today, not only in contemporary Christian music, but in folk and rock. Although guitar lessons are a good way to learn the basics, many people have learned to play the guitar with an instructional book that showed how to play chords, tune the instrument, and strum or pick the strings for different sounds. (Tip: Buy a pitch pipe at the music store to help tune your guitar.)

Instructional videos are an excellent way to get a good start on learning to play chords. These videos are available at music stores, video rental stores, and even public libraries. Look for a good guitar, either classical (last three strings are nylon) or acoustic (all steel strings). You might rent an instrument at first to see if your child is going to stick with it. (This is a good idea when considering any expensive musical instrument for your child.) If you know someone who plays the guitar, have him go with you to find the best instrument for the price. Half-size guitars are available for and helpful to young children. Ask for the right how-to-play book for your child's age.

In order to learn guitar, a child needs to be at least seven or eight years old with good finger and motor coordination, a self-starter, and motivated enough to practice daily to improve the sound he can make. But in a short time, after learning a few chords, he can sing his first songs and accompany himself on the guitar.

More easy-to-learn instruments, with videos, audiocassettes, or instructional books, are also available for:

Keyboard. Check a music store or toy store. Often the keyboard comes with instructions and songbook. There are many different sizes, brands, and price ranges. See the end of this chapter for information on synthesizers, keyboards, and computer software.

Lap Harp. From preschoolers up, everyone can learn to play a simple wooden lap harp with the follow-the-dot song sheets that slip underneath the strings for easy learning. Your child can play many musical styles on the harp. Although your child won't learn to read music, the lap harp is a great way to practice rhythms and play and sing familiar songs or even make up new tunes. No reading is required.

Xylophone or Marimba. This instrument has a series of hard wooden bars, played by being struck with small hammers. It is good for people of any age in learning rhythm and simple melodies.

Autoharp. This is a good instrument for older children and adults. With an autoharp and instructional book, you can strum and make chords to accompany singing.

When your child learns one of these instruments well enough to play a few songs, get a blank tape and cassette recorder and let her record a performance of her recorder, guitar, keyboard, or harp music. Friends who play instruments could contribute to the music on the cassette tape.

COMMUNITY RESOURCES FOR MUSIC LESSONS

If private lessons are out of financial reach, most cities and even small towns provide community resources. YMCAs and community centers can offer affordable group lessons—in piano, guitar, trumpet, or any instrument—in their summer, weekend, or after-school programs. If they don't, make the suggestion and offer to help find a teacher.

Group lessons offer many benefits. They are much less expensive; it is motivating for a child to play with his peers; and the interaction between teacher and students as they make music together is great. Look for Yamaha and Suzuki group lessons also (see appendix A for a description of these methods).

Churches can invest in Orff instruments and give children the opportunity to play in an Orff ensemble (see appendix A), sing in children's choirs, play in bell choirs, and perform their own musical productions.

SCHOOL RESOURCES FOR MUSIC LESSONS

When you are choosing a new school for your child, ask what music instruction is included in the school day. Elementary schools offer lessons in most types of instruments. Some even provide piano lessons as one option in their curriculum. Junior high and high schools have orchestras, bands, and music ensembles in which your teenager can participate. This school instruction costs a minimal fee or nothing at all, and you can rent the instrument by the month. If the school your child attends cannot afford a full- or part-time music teacher, find a parent volunteer who's willing to give lessons or direct a choir or small band.

MUSIC, COMPUTERS, AND KEYBOARDS

We are not well informed these days about music unless we have learned something about computers. And the computer realm has much to offer in the area of musical pleasure, creation, and instruction.

Hardware

The kind of computer to buy will depend on what functions you have in mind. Music software is available for PCs, as well as for Macintosh (at this time, the leader in music software). Many organizations promote the educational uses of computers. In the home, with the use of the many software programs available, a computer can be used for teaching nearly all aspects of music theory, for composition, for sequencing, and for notation, from elementary through advanced levels.

Software

Since software changes almost daily, any listing here would be incomplete. Keeping in touch with software companies or finding someone in your community who uses software (local public school music teachers or an organization supporting computer education—check your local library) will help. Music software for the computer can be designed for the computer only or for a MIDI (an acronym for musical instrument digital interface) instrument (probably a keyboard) and a MIDI interface. If the software is advertised as MIDI software, it will require a MIDI instrument and interface.

Software Companies. For an up-to-date listing of music software and hardware and for information and support for your questions about computer music, visit www.computersandmusic.com. You can also e-mail questions and obtain technical support from Computers and Music, 4837 Geary Blvd., San Francisco, CA 94118. Phone: 800-767-6161; e-mail: compmus @well.com.

Keyboards. There are many keyboards available, from those in the department or discount store, to very expensive ones from your music dealer. You can also find used ones advertised in the classified sections of newspapers and electronic music magazines. Here are a few suggestions:

1. Be sure you get a keyboard that is MIDI compatible.
2. Make sure the key width and octave distance is the same as that of an acoustic piano if you plan to use it for piano practice.
3. Be sure the sounds are good. You will probably end up liking a few, but you will tire of them quickly if they are thin, distorted, and too unrealistic. Remember that music is an aural skill, and sound is extremely important. This is one of the crucial areas that separate the less expensive from the more expensive keyboards.
4. Weighted action is important, especially if the keyboard will be used for piano practice. Some keyboards have an adjustable feature that can make the action heavier or lighter.
5. Many keyboards have sixty-one or fewer keys. A full-sized keyboard has eighty-eight keys. Again, if the keyboard is being used for piano practice, sixty-one keys will be frustrating.

When you buy a keyboard, you get what you pay for. I have not listed all the features that are available. Stay away from the less expensive keyboards if you plan to use it for more than a toy.

A MUSIC FESTIVAL: MAKING AND PLAYING YOUR OWN INSTRUMENTS

Get your friends and family together to make instruments and have a rhythm music festival. After making the instruments, you can:

- decorate the instruments with stickers, paint, markers
- take turns being the conductor and directing the musicians when to stop and start playing and how loud or soft to play
- play familiar children's songs on your audiocassette recorder, and players can chime, tap, or strum along with their instruments
- invite one of your friends who already knows how to play a recorder, guitar, or other instrument to play with you
- have a musical parade outdoors, with the leader jumping, hopping, or doing whatever movement he chooses as the others follow and imitate, while playing their instruments

After you've made plenty of music, have cookies and lemonade or juice and celebrate!

Instruments to Make for Your Music Festival

Bamboo flutes. Cut bamboo sticks into four or five different, graduated lengths. Each piece must have a knot in it that seals off the air. If there is a hole in the bamboo piece, seal it with a bit of gum or florist clay. Then set the bamboo sticks next to each other in order of size and wrap masking tape around the four or five bamboo sticks to hold them steady. With a little practice, you can make a nice sound by blowing into the different sections of your bamboo flute.

Kazoos. They're fun to play and easy to make. Use a clean comb. Cut a strip of waxed paper the length of the comb. Hold the strip tightly across the teeth of your comb. Now you're ready to blow a tune against your teeth.

Homemade guitar. Take a shoebox, and put five or six rubber bands around it. Rubber bands of different thickness make different sounds. Decorate your guitar with markers or stickers. Plink out a song.

Sandpaper blocks. These make a great percussion instrument for your neighborhood orchestra. Get two blocks of thick wood from a local builder or a construction project (asking for permission to use wood if there is extra), or from a builder's supply store. Secure sandpaper all the way around the wood with thumbtacks. Rub the blocks together to make a scraping noise.

Coat-hanger chimes. With string, hang different things (tiny clay pot, several sizes and types of kitchen spoons, a big nail, etc.) to the horizontal part of a wire coat hanger. Using a thin dowel stick, tap out a tune on your chimes.

Also see rhythm instruments for younger children in the toddler section of "Your Child's Musical Development," chapter 4.

Chapter Six

Music Games and Activities

Sing to it, play, work and dance to it,
Love and reminisce where, why, and when.

GABRIELLA

M om, how do you play Musical Chairs? I forgot…. And do you remember Name That Tune? Didn't we play that in the car going to Grandma's once?"

Kids love to play games, and they most often rely on big sisters and brothers, parents and grandparents to pass down the games they know and to show them the rules or ways to play. Music games are part of the sheer fun of being young (and young at heart). They often combine singing or chanting with jumping or dancing and thus stimulate children's musical development. So some of the games that follow are just for fun.

With so many manufactured games—video, computer games, and electronic toys—many kids today are not growing up knowing how to play the old games that involve music, movement, and lots of fun. Activities with music can be an enjoyable way to reinforce things children have learned or to teach new skills and concepts. Whether you are a parent who wants to have fun with your kids, a homeschool mom who wants to integrate music into daily learning, or a teacher who desires to bring more music into your classroom and use musical games to teach, you will find games and activities in this chapter that will help a child learn a variety of skills. He will have opportunities for movement, learn the music alphabet and notation, and more. Here are a few ideas to get you started. At the end of this chapter, resources are listed to help you discover more music games.

WHO, ME?

Purpose: to learn memory skills, reaction timing, and rhythm

No equipment is required, and the game can be played anywhere. Five to a dozen players can participate. Choose a leader. The leader assigns numbers, letters, or names to each of the other players, and players memorize their numbers as well as other players' numbers. Then the leader sets up a clapping rhythm and it is followed by all the other players. The leader starts the chant, and players continue in rhythm.

> Leader: "Number 5."
> Number 5: "Who, me?"
> Leader: "Yes, you."
> Number 5: "Couldn't be."
> Leader: "Then, who?"
> Number 5: "Number 3."
> Number 3: "Who, me?"
> Leader: "Yes, you."
> Number 3: "Couldn't be."
> Leader: "Then, who?"
> Number 3: "Number 1."

And so the game continues with the pace of the rhythm, questions, and answers getting faster until players make mistakes. When the wrong response (or no response) is given, a player is out for the round. Play continues until there is only one player left to answer the leader's question. He or she is the winner.

MUSICAL CHAIRS

Purpose: fun and alertness

For decades, Musical Chairs has been a favorite game with children. Most of us have played it at our birthday parties. Both small and large groups can enjoy this game. All you need is someone to operate a radio or tape player or to play an instrument. Line chairs up back to back, forming two rows, or in a circle with seats facing outward, with one chair less than the number of participants. While the music is played, the players parade around the edge of the chairs. As soon as the music stops, players scurry to be seated in the closest chair. The child left without a seat is out of the game. Then one chair is removed, and the music starts again while the players parade around the chairs. When the music stops, everyone tries to get a seat. The game continues until only one chair and two players are left. To soften the blow of being out on the round of musical chairs, you could hand each player a treat as he leaves the game.

NAME THAT TUNE

Purpose: to recall familiar tunes and sing them

This is a good game to play while traveling in the car. The first player hums or whistles several measures of a tune, while the other players try to guess what it is. The player who guesses the right song gets to be "It" and sing or hum the next tune.

LONDON BRIDGE

Purpose: to develop singing, skipping, and running skills

This old-fashioned game has been a favorite of children for generations, yet many people have forgotten how to play it. At least eight players are needed. Two players are chosen to be the bridge keepers, and they link hands together above their heads to form an arch through which the other players will run or skip. The players line up in pairs, and as everyone sings the verses to the song, the pairs of players run or skip through the bridge and then back to the end of the line to go through the bridge again. Sometime during the words of the verse "Take the keys and lock them up," the bridge keepers lower their arms and capture the pair of players trying to pass through. Those players should try to scurry through when they feel the bridge is about to lower.

When a pair of players is caught, one player stands behind one bridge keeper, and the other player stands behind the other bridge keeper. The song is sung again and again until all players have been caught and are on the two equal teams. Then the two teams play tug of war to select the winning team.

Here are the words of "London Bridge." (You can make up your own verses.)

London Bridge is falling down, falling down, falling down.
London Bridge is falling down, my fair lady.
How shall we build it up again, up again, up again?
How shall we build it up again, my fair lady?
We will build with wood and clay, wood and clay, wood and
    clay.
We will build with wood and clay, my fair lady.
But wood and clay will wash away, wash away, wash away.
Wood and clay will wash away, my fair lady.
We will build with silver and gold, silver and gold, silver and
    gold.
We will build with silver and gold, my fair lady.
But silver and gold will be stolen away, stolen away, stolen
    away.
Silver and gold will be stolen away, my fair lady.
We'll put a man to watch all night, watch all night, watch all
    night.
We'll put a man to watch all night, my fair lady.
Suppose the man should fall asleep, fall asleep, fall asleep.
Suppose the man should fall asleep, my fair lady.
Take the keys and lock him up, lock him up, lock him up.
Take the keys and lock him up, my fair lady.

BINGO GAMES

Purpose: to become familiar with music words and symbols

Make some bingo cards with music symbols or words printed on them. Terms or definitions are read by a leader, and the players mark the squares that match. Other aspects of music can be taught by putting different information on the cards.

MEMORY GAMES

Purpose: to become familiar with music words

Make a memory game using music words. Create a total of forty cards using twenty different words (see vocabulary list in chapter 10), two cards for each word. (You can increase the number of cards as your music vocabulary expands.) One card has the word and one the definition. Put all the cards face down on the table or floor. Each player gets to turn over two cards. If he finds a match, he keeps those cards and gets to turn over two more cards. Continue until all cards have been turned over and matched. The winner is the player with the most pairs of cards.

Word Searches

Purpose: to become familiar with music words

Make up a word search, including names and/or events from vocabulary lists, composers' names, and events. Limit each word search to one topic if possible. Make a grid with spaces for fifteen letters across and twenty letters down. Fill in approximately ten to twelve words, going vertically, horizontally, or diagonally. Words can be written forward or backward. Fill in other spaces with random letters. To play, color the words you find with a highlighter.

Tempo Games

Purpose: to learn tempo directions

Make cards with the various tempo words taken from the vocabulary listings of Month 10 in chapter 10: Johannes Brahms. Place them in order from slowest to fastest. Mix them up and try to put them in the correct order (largo, lento, adagio, andante, moderato, allegro, vivace, presto).

Singing Games

Purpose: to develop aural and singing skills
- Sing everyday communications (questions, phone numbers, prayers, etc.), and have the child respond by singing.
- Sing two pitches, and have the child repeat.
- As the child increases in competence, gradually increase the length of the melody to three notes, then four, etc., and have him or her repeat.
- Sing songs to the child at bedtime and anytime.
- Teach songs to the child regularly.

FUN WITH MOVEMENT AND RHYTHM

Purpose: to develop rhythmic skills

Make rhythm instruments out of materials you have at home, for example:

- *drums* from round oatmeal or other hot-cereal container
- *shakers* from rice in a plastic container with tight lid
- *rattles* from popcorn (kernels) in a hard-surfaced plastic container with a tight lid
- *clackers* from two wooden spoons

(Use your imagination regarding what you have at home, or you can buy premade instruments.) Then use the instruments in the following ways.

- Have your child beat time to music. Begin with something that is very rhythmic (marches, etc.), then work up to pieces with more subtle rhythms.
- Have your child march to music. Progress from very rhythmic to subtly rhythmic pieces.
- Do exercises to music. Use action songs.

LEARNING INTERVALS

Purpose: to learn the music alphabet, direction, and intervals (distance between note names)

Make two (or more) sets of cards with A B C D E F G printed on them. (You can use a toy xylophone with letters or a piano keyboard with letters temporarily affixed to the middle area of the keys.)

1. Arrange them in order to go up or higher in pitch.
2. Arrange them backward to go down or lower in pitch.
3. Arrange them going up or down in intervals. (See vocabulary in Month 11 of chapter 10: Camille Saint-Saëns.)

   2nds (letters in order, up or down; for example, C to D = 2nd)
   3rds (skipping a letter, up or down; for example, C to E = 3rd)
   4ths (skipping two letters, up or down; C to F = 4th)
   5ths (skipping three letters, up or down; C to G = 5th)
   6ths (skipping four letters, up or down; C to A = 6th)
   7ths (skipping five letters, up or down; C to B = 7th)
   8ths (skipping six letters, up or down; C to C = 8th)

4. Parent or leader calls out instructions ("Up a third from C," or "Down a fifth from D"), and others arrange two appropriate cards.
5. Sing the intervals. Play them first on an instrument, then sing.

BEANBAG GAMES

Purpose: to learn to read music notation

Make a large grand staff with treble and bass clefs (lines should be three inches apart). Make bean bags about three inches in diameter.

Example: Staff

Play games with grand staff (on floor) and beanbags:

- Toss a beanbag onto the grand staff, then name the pitch wherever the bag has landed.
- Use beanbags to make intervals.
- Use beanbags to note familiar songs.

GAMES FOR NOTE VALUES

Purpose: to learn some of the different kinds of note values (See vocabulary in Month 9 in chapter 10: Robert Schumann.)

- Make flashcards with a note on one side and the number of counts it gets on the back of the card.
- Make large notes (head three inches in diameter) and cut them out (make at least four "quarter notes," two "half notes," one "whole note," eight "eighth notes," two "dots"). Place them on the grand staff on different lines and/or spaces.
- Name the pitch.
- Arrange in a short tune.

QUIZZES

Purpose: to reinforce general music information

- Make up true/false, multiple choice, or fill-in-the-blank quizzes over any of the material you have covered. Give satisfying praise and rewards for completing them.
- Find pictures of composers or instruments, and have players identify them.
- Play recordings. Have child identify title, composer, meter, etc., as he or she becomes more proficient.

SPINNER GAME

Purpose: to reinforce general music information

Use an old round pizza board divided into six or more parts with an arrow attached for spinning. The player takes a spin and recites whatever is requested. For example: names of notes, note values, meter, composer information, etc.

MUSIC PICTIONARY

Purpose: to reinforce general music information

Each team has twenty-five pieces of paper with words or terms on them. The players rotate, picking a term out of a hat and trying to draw the symbol to match for their team to guess. Keep a record of how fast each team finishes to challenge the next game. Examples for papers: composer names, names of notes, rhythms, etc.

CREATE A SONG

Purpose: to develop aural and playing and singing skills

Each team is given eight separated measures of a familiar song with notes, rests, etc. on them. Each team member gets to play or sing his or her measure(s). All team members try to guess the song and put the measures in the correct order.

RHYTHM RACE

Purpose: to reinforce various rhythm patterns

Make a stack of cards with different rhythms on them. Each player goes through the stack one at a time and chants, claps, or plays the rhythm. Each player is timed, and his or her name is put on a rhythm chart for the month.

MUSIC COLLAGE OF THE MONTH

Purpose: to reinforce general music information

Create a music collage from old magazines or homemade symbols, and see if the player can identify everything in it.

YES OR NO?

Purpose: to reinforce general music information

Composers' names, symbols, or songs are put on note cards, and one is taped to each player's back. Each player must ask yes-or-no questions of the group and try to discover what is written on the card taped to his or her back.

EASTER EGG HUNT

Purpose: to reinforce general music information

Hide colored plastic Easter eggs with terms or questions inside. Use a point system for different colored eggs. Each player gets points for each egg collected and an extra ten points if he or she can answer the question in the egg. This game could be modified for other times of the year by hiding music symbols (different note values made out of construction paper).

FLASHCARD RELAY

Purpose: to reinforce knowledge of musical notes

Each child says the name of the note on the flashcard and plays it on the piano (or other pitched instrument). Each team will be timed to see who is the fastest.

HOLIDAY DART GAME

Purpose: to reinforce general music information

Draw a picture and section it off. Write directions in each section. Using a dart gun, players shoot the picture and receive extra practice points for following the directions in the section they hit. For example:

October: picture of a pumpkin
November: picture of a turkey
December: picture of a Christmas tree

COMPOSER BIRTHDAYS

Purpose: to reinforce information about famous composers

Celebrate composer birthdays with the family or group of children. Have a cake and candles. See the "Time Line of Selected Composers" for dates.

COMPOSER VIDEO

Purpose: to provide a creative way to study composers' lives

A family, more than one family, or a group of children choose a composer, write a drama about his life, and film it, using music of the composer in the background.

MUSIC WITH WATER GLASSES

Purpose: to experiment with sounds and pitches

Arrange approximately eight water glasses in a row, and add water to each, starting at the left with the lowest amount and increasing the amount in each glass as you move to the right. Gently tap each glass with a soft mallet, and listen to the sounds. Gently tap with a harder mallet, and listen. Listen to the pitches: From left to right would be low to high. The glasses can be tuned so that each glass represents a scale note. For example, the white keys on the piano from C up to the next C can be created by changing water levels in the glasses, and then songs like "Mary Had a Little Lamb" can be played. This game requires close supervision.

The books listed below provide additional ideas and materials. Peruse children's activity books in stores and libraries for more musical games.

Athey, Margaret, and Gwen Hitchkiss. *A Galaxy of Games for the Music Class.* New York: Parker Publishing, 1975. This book contains 241 imaginative games and teacher aids for communicating the major principles of music theory and appreciation, using rhythmic response, melody writing, music notation, and ear training. Parents should have some music background in order to use this book.

Wirth, Marian, and others. *Musical Games, Fingerplays and Rhythmic Activities for Early Childhood.* New York: Parker Publishing, 1983. With its 224 pages of clearly defined games that include singing, moving, chanting, and listening, this is an excellent source for parents with young children.

Yurko, Michiko. *No H in Snake: Music Therapy for Children.* Van Nuys, Calif.: Alfred Publishing, 1979. This Suzuki-based book contains 271 pages of creative ways to teach different aspects of music, such as lines and spaces, clefs, pitches, scales, and key signatures, along with patterns for making instructional materials.

Chapter Seven

The Joy of Movement

Would you like to swing on a star;
Carry moonbeams home in a jar;
And be better off than you are?
Or would you rather be a fish?

TRADITIONAL FOLK SONG

Along with immersing our children in music, one of the biggest favors we can do for them is to include musical movement as a part of our family life. We're all born with a love for song and dance, but as we grow older (especially if there's no opportunity to move and make music), many lose the spark or forget how to dance a happy jig. We can rediscover the joys of music and movement with our children.

WAYS TO INCORPORATE MUSICAL MOVEMENT INTO FAMILY LIFE AND THE CLASSROOM

- Introduce musical movement to infants by putting on soothing classical or lullaby music. Start swaying or rocking to the steady beat of the music. When the baby of Oklahoma music teacher Pam Bradford was crying with colic, Pam put on peaceful music, held her baby in her arms, moved gently to the music, and found that it really calmed her down.
- Dance across the room with your babies from an early age to help them feel the steady pulse of the music. A strong sense of rhythm is an

essential foundation for the development of physical coordination, and it is necessary when the child takes music lessons later on.

- When you read nursery rhymes to a child, bounce her gently in your arms or on your lap to the steady pulse of rhyme and rhythm.

- When you sing a song, take a favorite stuffed animal and have the animal bounce the beat. Children love this, and it aids their developing sense of rhythm. A lively folk or children's song like "Froggy Went a Courtin'," "Rub-A-Dub," or "Baa Baa Black Sheep" is perfect for this activity.

- As soon as children can stand and walk, circle games are delightful movement fun. Get a big stuffed animal, and set it between you and the children. By joining hands, you can do a simple musical circle game, such as "Ring a Ring of Roses," "Sally Go Round the Sun," or "The Gallant Ship." (See public library for books that contain words and music to many children's and traditional folk songs. Also see the resources listed in appendix B, including John Feierabend's *Music for Little People* and *Music for Very Little People,* and suggestions at the end of this chapter, which are excellent resources for simple songs children and parents can dance and move to.) Do whatever motions the song suggests: jump up and down, fall at the end, or sink like a ship. Singing and doing movements with the music provide an element of fun.

- Help children notice and appreciate the everyday rhythms all around us: the tick of a clock, falling rain, bells ringing in church, drums in a parade, your feet as you hop, skip, run, or walk.

- Play some different types of music on a CD or audiocassette, and see if the children can skip, gallop, sway, or jump to the music.

- Try different types of structured circle games in which you go to the right, go to the left, step in, and step out like "Way Down Yonder in the Paw Paw Patch" or "Old Brass Wagons."

- When children are in first or second grade, move on to circle games that require the participants to keep a steady beat and follow directions, as in "Did You Ever See a Lassie?" "Hokey Pokey," and "Old Brass Wagon"; these are fun to learn and great group activities. They contain easy square-dance movements that help children continue to develop coordination, rhythm, and cooperation.

- If you know a favorite kind of dance from your family's cultural heritage or your musical background, put on the music and dance with the children, just for fun. Let them move along with you in your arms or, if they're old enough, teach them the necessary steps to do the dance: waltz, polka, or Israeli dance. Even preschoolers can learn simple Israeli dances with their clapping, rhythmic stepping, and snapping to the music.

- Put on the "Nutcracker Suite," let your little boy wear a soldier costume and your little girl wear a tutu or ballerina costume you found at a garage sale, and dance to the music. This is pure delight for little ones.
- If school-age children show interest, lessons in jazz, tap, ballet, or modern dancing are valuable. In addition, group lessons at a local dance studio, YMCA, after-school recreational center, or summer program can be a wonderful activity and less expensive than private dance lessons. Take children to a ballet or musical theater production that includes a variety of dance styles.

FOLK DANCING

What do the English Contra, Dutch Clogging, and Israeli Ma Navu have in common? They are all folk dances—the social dance of a particular nation or group. Throughout history, almost every culture and country has developed its own folk dances. A major event at ethnic folk festivals throughout this and other countries, folk dancing is a wonderful form of entertainment and exercise, and it's a way for people to celebrate and maintain the culture of their past.

Folk dancing has many benefits for the parents, teachers, and children who participate. Besides being fun to do, it's great physical exercise (many dances are so lively they burn as many calories as aerobic dancing) and a good way for kids to let off steam constructively. Folk dancing develops children's spatial awareness, rhythm, and coordination.

Folk dancing is intergenerational, with older generations teaching the younger ones. It is a marvelous group activity for parents, children, and even grandparents to engage in, providing family members an opportunity to do something fun together.

Folk dancers learn to cooperate and follow directions. They gain a sense of belonging. Unlike sports, where you may be the last one picked to play on the team or have to sit on the bench, folk dancing is inclusive, giving everyone a chance to participate, and there's no need for partners. It offers friendship and wholesome exercise for kids. It's also a good activity to include in elementary-school physical education programs.

Folk dancing has been around since the first groups of immigrants came to this country, but these days it is experiencing a little revival in America. Schools and churches are beginning to sponsor folk dance nights once a month or more often and are finding it a great family activity. At one such event in a Connecticut community, parents and children come to the elementary school gymnasium once a month for "Family Folk Dancing" and do simple folk dances. Volunteers teach beginners the dances. Everyone participates. This has been so successful that it has grown into the Family Chorus, a choir made up of youngsters and their parents.

In our city an International Folk Dance group meets every Monday night at a local church. From seven to eight o'clock veteran dancers teach beginners dances from Greece, Israel, England, China, Taiwan, Russia, Mexico, Africa, and the American South. All ages—children to senior citizens—are welcome, and participants from many different ethnic groups and walks of life come to enjoy fellowship and fun.

A friend in our church, Bob Burrall, started folk dancing in 1986 after seeing Israeli dancing in a Christmas musical production of *Amahl and the Night Visitors*. The dancers told him about a synagogue where people met regularly to do Israeli dancing. Bob then connected with the International Folk Dance group. "I've made friendships with all kinds of different people from different ethnic backgrounds," says Bob. "I've learned a lot about different cultures and enjoy the exercise and performances we've done at local festivals."

Bob's heritage is German, so he loved learning German dances and wearing the national costume, lederhosen, short leather pants held up by broad leather suspenders with a brightly decorated band across the chest, knee socks, and green hat. He has danced at the Oktoberfest in the fall and at other folk-dancing events.

Bob finds Israeli dancing spiritually uplifting and has had opportunities to teach children at Vacation Bible School and Dutch festivals how to folk dance.

Where Can You Find Folk Dancing in Your Community?

A good place to look for folk-dancing events is in your local newspaper. Folk-dancing festivals are often announced in the entertainment section. From "Red Earth," a big Native-American festival held in our city each year that includes Native-American food, dancing, and crafts, to the Greek Orthodox Church festival held annually and the Czech festival and Polka Contest in nearby Yukon, Oklahoma, our community and nearly every one in America has such folk-dancing events.

Another good way to locate folk-dancing groups is to call local ethnic churches. From there you will find other connections. If you go to a festival, you can ask the dancers about local folk-dancing groups. When you travel, look for festivals along the way that feature folk dances. In the summer there are festivals in many places in the United States where you can observe international dancing.

Folk-dancing groups sponsor seminars several times a year where you can learn new dances and how to teach them.

Ways to Share Folk Dancing with Your Children

- After you have learned a few folk dances, throw a party in your backyard, and teach your child and neighborhood children easy dances like a Mexican Carnavalito, an Israeli Zemer Atik dance, or others, and serve refreshments.
- Discover and learn a dance from your family's cultural background. Serve food from that cuisine. Look in music stores and libraries for information about your heritage.
- When your child's social studies or geography class studies a particular country, encourage the teacher to include learning a folk dance from that country, or offer to teach one yourself. Learning a native folk dance and the meaning of the steps helps the students understand the people and their culture. For further enrichment, the class can take a field trip to a Scottish festival, Indian powwow, clogging festival, or other folk events in your community.
- Encourage your local YMCA, recreation center, or elementary school to sponsor a "Family Folk-Dancing Night" once a month. A good resource for instructors to lead such an activity is Phyllis Weikart's videotapes, cassettes, and books with an easy-access approach to teaching and learning international folk dances: *Teaching Movement and Dance: A Sequential Approach to Rhythmic Movement,* 3d ed. with CD and videos available, High/Scope Press, 600 North River Street, Ypsilanti, MI 48198-2898.

Also, check your library (including children's section and audio/video departments), teacher's resource store, or music stores for other resources on international and American folk dancing.

Here are some audio and video dance resources for children and parents:

Artichokes and Brussels Sprouts. Activity and story songs by Fran Avni, a Canadian preschool educator and music specialist. Lyrics enclosed for jazz, march, classical, bluegrass, and reggae songs that are fun to dance to.

Dance Along. Sesame Street home video for ages three to twelve, where kids learn Big Bird's, Grover's, and the Sesame Street group's favorite dances.

Dancin' Magic by Joanie Bartels, for ages four to twelve. A cassette that will get both children and parents dancing the Hokey Pokey, polka, and Peppermint Twist.

Shake It to the One That You Love the Best: Play Songs and Lullabies from Black Musical Traditions. An award-winning audiocassette and songbook with a joyful collection of songs from African, African-American, Creole, and Caribbean cultures—in jazz, reggae, gospel, rhythm and blues, and classical styles—that kids will hop up and sing and dance to.

This is just a sampling of the many videos, audiocassettes, and dance instruction books and songbooks that can be found at children's bookstores, teacher/parent learning resource stores, music stores, church, school, and public libraries, and catalogs, such as *Music for Little People* (800-757-2233).

Part Three

Music in Our World

Chapter Eight

Music Styles in Our American Culture

Children raised on good culture are better at resisting crass popular culture.

CHUCK COLSON

All of us are affected daily by many styles of music. When I walk into a certain dress shop in the mall, I hear contemporary French rock music blaring from the speakers. Music of all kinds serves as background—though in many places too loud to be merely background—as we eat in restaurants. Movies and television programs are woven through with musical soundtracks. Even while driving down the street I am confronted with rap or rock music booming out of the speakers in the car next to mine.

It is impossible to escape the music of the surrounding culture, short of wearing earplugs and staying home. How then can we as families deal with the music of our culture? How can we enjoy different styles of music—country and Western, folk, reggae, and rap? And how can parents deal with the music that attracts their children and teenagers?

We must approach this subject with intelligence and information. So let's describe some current styles of music.

Country and Western

Also referred to merely as country music, this began as the traditional music of the rural southern United States. It was first heard among pioneers during the 1800s in Kentucky, North and South Carolina, West Virginia, and Tennessee, but by the 1940s the popularity of country music had spread through the United States and abroad. In its beginnings, country and Western music was influenced by English, Irish, and Scottish ballads brought to this country by immigrants and was combined with the blues music of southern African Americans. It was simple and told a story. Today's country music blends rock and popular music with traditional tunes and themes and uses acoustic and steel guitar, fiddle, bass, drums, piano, and keyboard. The heart and headquarters of C&W is Nashville, where the Grand Ole Opry literally made the stardom of singers such as Patsy Cline, Conway Twitty, and Loretta Lynn. An additional center of country music has sprung up over recent years in Branson, Missouri, where audiences farther west can enjoy live stage shows and concerts year round.

Folk

The early folk songs were passed from person to person and across generations in the oral tradition; some originated from English or Scottish roots. Most early folk songs were ballads having simple words and music with no instrumental accompaniment; instrumental parts were added later. The verses tell a story, and the chorus is usually repeated. Early American folk songs were about family life, religious faith, hard work, and surviving loneliness and poverty.[1]

During the 1950s, singers such as Woody Guthrie and Pete Seeger gained acclaim performing American folk songs. The themes began to shift to social problems such as racial prejudice and the need for peace. With singers such as Bob Dylan and Joan Baez in the late 1960s, folk music became "folk-rock" and was immensely popular. Today's folk music employs guitar, banjo, harmonica, violin, and sometimes dulcimers and mandolins. Folk festivals occur regularly all over the United States, many of them regional.

Pop-Dance/Rock

Rock-'n'-roll music came out of mixing rhythm and blues with country music, and the style gained popularity in the 1950s with performers like Elvis Presley, Jerry Lee Lewis, Chuck Berry, Fats Domino, and others.[2]

Although pop—or Top 40—music of today's teens has an electronic, synthesized sound, much of it focuses on love and romance as did early rock music. As Al Menconi says, it promotes "that swooning sensation—the right combination of soaring feelings, reeling senses, and hyperactive hormones that is proof positive that you're in love."[3] The difference, Menconi points out, between the early rock music and today's is that some of today's leans "toward more graphic sexuality, multiple partners, adultery, and even kinky sex and sadomasochism."[4]

Rock music also ranges from heavy metal, party metal, and hardcore metal to alternative music groups and techno music. For discussions of these and other types of rock music affecting today's young people, see *Plugged In,* a magazine published by Focus on the Family (see appendix B).

Rap

Rap originated from the talking styles of African-American culture and later the "talking jazz" of the 1950s and 1960s. Closely related to hip-hop, rap developed into the sound of black urban youth. It is a "chanted rhyme backed by the rhythms of a beat box—either human or mechanical."[5]

Its themes range from boasting and sexual conquest, to the grimmer realities of gang and street life, drugs, and violence. Rap also expresses the resurgence of black cultural pride and nationalism and includes Christian rap. Rap first gained popularity among young people in African-American and Hispanic neighborhoods in New York City in the 1970s. But by the mid-1980s, rap hit the mainstream and became the big musical trend that crossed races, not only in the United States but all over the world.[6]

Reggae

Reggae music originated in Jamaica. Characterized by its slow, rhythmic tempo that utilizes bongos, guitars, bass, and electric guitar, reggae music gained widespread popularity in the late 1980s and 1990s. Instead of lyrics about love, traditional reggae features revolutionary themes with a message about the condition of black people in Jamaica or the United States. Songs like Bob Marley's "Stir It Up," "Buffalo Soldier," or "Steel Posts" on albums *Earth Crisis* and *State of Emergency* urge people to wake up and throw off oppression.

International Styles

As the world has become a global village, Americans have enjoyed greater access to the music of Russia and Eastern Europe, Japan, Africa, and Latin America. The growing ethnic diversity of our nation contributes to the variety of music styles now available to us. When Thomas, a foreign exchange student from Germany, lived in our home for a semester, we heard German techno-music, a synthesized, dance-rhythm sound that is very popular with teenagers in Eastern Europe. Although it was not my cup of tea, it was interesting to taste the musical favorites of our international guest.

Attending ethnic festivals in the community is a good way to hear music from other cultures: Mexican-American celebrations, Greek Orthodox church festivals, and festivals of Scottish, Amish, Czech, and German populations. Many ethnic restaurants will play recorded music from the country of origin or even have ensembles perform. And in most music stores, there is a section of international music.

How Can Your Family Decide What Is Appropriate for Your Children and Teens to Listen To?

When you expose your child to the wonderful variety of music available today, you are helping develop a taste in your child for quality music. As Ann Manley, a mother and youth director in Oklahoma City, says, "I've tried to take my children to Michael W. Smith concerts and terrific Broadway musicals that come to town like *Les Misérables* and *Phantom of the Opera*. We've got to pay the price to expose our kids to the excitement of Christian concerts and quality musicals to create a love for good music and the theater."

When it comes to instilling solid values in our children, it is tempting to declare non-Christian music off-limits. While that may protect children from destructive themes, it will not teach them to develop the ability to discriminate between good and bad music. Is good music merely that which has lyrics that are scriptural or that mention Jesus? What do you want your children to learn and apply about the use of vocal and dynamic ranges, proficiency on instruments, and creativity with rhythms and harmonies? Can they discover God's truth that emerges in the works of thinking and sensitive people, even if they are not Christian? What part can music play in building social awareness in your children? What clues can we find about the way nonbelievers think by listening to music of the culture?

Each family must set its own limits and standards. As in other moral areas, when our children are young, we apply stronger rules so that we can train them; as they grow up, however, the goal is to make fewer rules so that our children may grow into making wise choices on their own, using conscious, thoughtful judgments based on the truthful criteria they have developed.

If we truly want our children to bring Christ to their friends, at some point—by high school or college—they will gain much understanding about the philosophies and world-views of non-Christian friends by hearing what those friends are listening to and resonating with, just as we learn about other philosophies and religions sometime during our education. We must not eliminate the reasonable gathering of information that lies outside our Christian subculture. The difficult task is determining when the time is right for our children to be exposed to the nonbelieving world in these cultural areas.

But while we are setting standards and—we would hope—influencing the musical tastes of our children, here are some strategies to help us avoid panic, overreaction, or alienation.

Pray

Commit time as a couple or in your own personal devotional times to pray for wisdom and discernment, to bathe the current situation in prayer (as when your teenager brings home a CD you find offensive) before acting or reacting. Search the Scriptures for what guidance God's Word has for you and your family concerning entertainment, music, and movie guidelines, and what your limits should be.

Buy Music with Redeeming and Positive Messages on a Regular Basis

Music by Christians and having clearly Christian messages comes in many styles—country, folk, soul, rap, etc.—and it's one of the best investments you can make. Music from artists like Keith Green, Annie Herring, and Charlie Peacock that we bought for our family and listened to years ago was still a favorite with our kids in their teenage years. Fill your home and car with music that is uplifting, that will help you focus on what is right, pure, lovely, admirable, excellent, and praiseworthy (Philippians 4:8).

Be a Good Role Model in Your Choice of Listening Entertainment

It's hard to convince your teenager to abstain from heavy metal when he borrows your car and hears your CDs proclaiming the wonder of an extramarital affair. Young people see the inconsistency immediately.

If you enjoy a collection of music that lies outside the range of traditional artists, give your children clues as to what you like about the music. Maybe you admire Paul Simon's openness to other cultures and his ability to incorporate new rhythms and harmonies into his own work. Or you appreciate the high level of technical and expressive proficiency of a great jazz musician. And you are encouraged and warmed by Peter, Paul, and Mary's concert tour that focuses on the nation's children. As your kids see you discriminate and choose the good but discard the bad, they will learn how to do this for themselves.

Spend Time with Your Teenager (Lots of It)

Develop open lines of communication and occasionally ask a question when his favorite music is playing: How does that song make you feel? Why is it your favorite? Does it drag you down or lift you up? Does it make you think about important life issues? Does it give you hope or joy? How do you feel it affects your spiritual life?

In this way you can better understand what draws your son or daughter to a certain kind of music and what effect it has on him or her. As parents, we need to keep in mind that, during adolescence, our kids are experiencing an upheaval of emotions; it is not necessarily a bad thing if they are choosing music styles that reflect their turmoil (hence, the upsurge of Christian rock). During a talk several years ago on a Christian college campus, Al Menconi warned parents not to confuse *style* with *lyrical content* of the music. After all, truly Christian music cannot always be "nice" and mellow, for the Christian message is often an uncomfortable, unsettling one. When a song depicts Jesus rebuking hypocrisy or injustice, a mellow musical style is really not appropriate.

Have Family Discussions About Music

Talk with your children and teenagers about limits; talk about what music will not be allowed in your home and why. Music touches our spirits, and there may come a time when certain types of music are damaging the spirit of your home. Explain this to your children; don't dismiss it with, "Well, I can't stand that group—I think they're disgusting—so you can't listen to it."

We need to consider both lyrics (what is this song saying—what's the message?) and the music itself. One mother said, "If the music had an incessantly hammering beat that creates anxiety and nervousness in our kids, we avoided it." Each family is different, but we need to learn how family members are affected by the music that pervades our household.

Our friends the Sergeants managed by investing in lots of contemporary Christian music, listening to some country music at home, eliminating MTV, and staying involved and in close touch with their four teenagers. When they felt a song was questionable, they asked their children to listen to it with them and pay attention to the lyrics, which are usually provided in the cassette or CD cover, and ask, "What is this saying?" They discussed the message or the philosophy behind it and whether it fit their family's guidelines.

Another mom we know, Nancy, dealt with her teenager's music by helping him look at the lifestyles of the performers. When her son became preoccupied with rock music during seventh grade, he spent hours alone in his room before and after school listening to it. Although he had been very open with her before, he became uncommunicative, and rock music filled his ears via a Walkman or boom box everywhere he went. His mom decided they needed to discuss his music together.

"So I bought books on rock music that gave profiles of rock musicians and popular groups. I encouraged him to read about them," Nancy said. After reading about the lifestyles of his heroes, he decided to throw away his CDs and began listening to more Christian contemporary music. He started a Christian contemporary band with a few friends and influenced many of his classmates to live for Christ.

Al Menconi shared some good advice with me: "If your child is drawn to a certain kind of music, avoid condemning the style just because you don't like it. When your child is into a certain music and identifying with the musicians, and you condemn it, he feels rejected and thus you alienate him."

On a positive side, enjoy a variety of music as a family. Be discerning and alert to the attitudes, lyrics, and philosophy behind the music. Some country singers, for example, have positive family-centered themes in their songs. Some songs focus on country dancing like "Boot-Scootin' Boogie." But other country songs concern drowning your sorrows in alcohol because your lover left you.

We even need to be selective about "Christian" music. Just because a song quotes Scripture does not mean that its doctrine is sound. And we shouldn't overlook poor musicianship just because the message of the song is true. We want our kids to develop discerning taste in all forms of entertainment. "Let's teach our teens to be sensitive to both the message and the medium," says Chuck Colson. "We all enjoy the choruses derived from Christian folk and pop music: they can add a fresh touch to our worship services. But when the style of the music overwhelms the Christian message, there we have to draw the line."[7]

BROADWAY MUSICALS, MOVIES, AND VIDEOS

Do you remember walking out of a movie house or live theater production whistling or singing the hit tune? A major portion of today's music industry focuses on producing soundtracks and musical scores for movies and musical theater. There are many quality musical scores and movie soundtracks you and your children can enjoy together. Since many of these are available on CDs, you can inexpensively bring the joy of musical theater and the memorable songs of the screen to your family.

For example, the Broadway production of *Fiddler on the Roof,* the story of the poor Jewish milkman living in a village in Czarist Russia who had five unmarried daughters to support, has some unforgettable songs—"Matchmaker, Matchmaker," "If I Were a Rich Man," and others—that are uplifting in both lyrics and music. This theater production was one of the longest-running shows in Broadway history. It was then made into an effective and highly successful movie musical. You don't have to go to New York or Chicago to see it—you can rent the video and enjoy it with your kids.

The smash Broadway hit *Annie,* loved by children of all ages, was first on the stage and then became a popular movie. It has some terrific songs: "Tomorrow" and "It's a Hard Knock Life." Set in New York City in the 1930s, *Annie* is the story of a feisty, red-headed orphan who dreams of a happy life outside the dingy confines of the orphanage she lives in—and how her dream comes true. When our daughter Alison first saw *Annie* on the stage in our city, she wanted the cassette tape and learned all the songs.

If your community has a summer musical theater, find out the schedule and try to take your children to a live performance. Many theaters have special, inexpensive matinées for children—be sure and ask! It's worth investing in tickets for your children to see quality musical performances.

There are many "oldies but goldies" musicals on video that you can rent at a video store, such as Judy Garland's *Meet Me in St. Louis* and *An American in Paris,* the Academy Award–winning musical from 1951. *An American in Paris* features the choreography and dancing of Gene Kelly and memorable Gershwin songs like "Embraceable You," "I Got Rhythm," and "Love Is Here to Stay."

Oklahoma! the Rodgers and Hammerstein musical set in the early 1900s, has been one of the most successful musicals in theater history. The movie version won the Academy Award in 1955 for best sound recording.

Here are some more memorable Broadway musicals on video that have great songs:

White Christmas	*Beauty and the Beast*
Carousel	*The Unsinkable Molly Brown*
West Side Story	*My Fair Lady*
Mame	*South Pacific*
Hello Dolly	*The Lion King*

Movie Soundtracks and Songs

The musical soundtrack adds drama, suspense, romantic color, and humor to a movie. The composer is usually on the location of the movie set to absorb the mood, style, and themes of the movie. Then he composes music where it is particularly effective, such as during action scenes or romantic scenes, or at climactic points in the story. In some movies, the soundtrack is a backdrop woven throughout the action, characterization, and dialogue, such as in the film *The Mission* (one of our son Chris's favorite soundtracks). In others, such as *Sister Act,* gospel songs and songs from the 1950s were sung by the main characters, and music played an integral part in the entire production.

In the animated movie *Beauty and the Beast,* which won an Academy Award for best musical score, music is used to develop the plot and relationships between characters. But even more important for a movie directed toward a young audience, music makes the movie more appealing and invites attention. For example, when Pam's preschool daughters watched *Beauty and the Beast,* she noticed how distracted and uninterested they became when there was only dialogue. But music signals that something special is about to happen, such as when Belle enters the ballroom, wearing her beautiful yellow gown, and Angela Lansbury sings as the Beast and Belle begin to dance around the ballroom. At that point Pam's daughters were riveted to the screen and drawn back into the plot.

In *Beauty and the Beast,* music operates also as a *segue*—a musical term meaning "to get from one point or place to another"—and provides a smooth transition between scenes.

Toward the end of the movie, when all the townspeople decide to track down the Beast and destroy him, they head toward the castle. The music rises in volume and builds suspense as the mob nears the castle and then enters it. The music leads the audience to the climactic scene where the Beast, who appears to have a mortal wound from Gaston, is transformed into the prince. In this movie the music is an integral part of the presentation.

Here are some can't-miss old movies with great scores:

Doctor Zhivago

Breakfast at Tiffany's: Audrey Hepburn starred in this memorable movie with its Oscar-winning score and song "Moon River."

*Amadeus: The film version of the London and Broadway stage play centers around Wolfgang Amadeus Mozart's life and music and includes many of his works. This is a good vehicle for introducing youngsters to what opera is all about and how an opera is conceived.

Chariots of Fire: It is based on the true story of a Christian athlete who became an Olympic star.

*The Last of the Mohicans: A recent remake based on James Fenimore Cooper's classic novel, it has an outstanding soundtrack.

The Sound of Music: This also is based on the story of a real family who lived in Austria during World War II.

(*Violent scenes and some profanity make these unadvisable for small and sensitive children.)

Children particularly enjoy the songs and musical scores from these movies:

Fantasia

The Jungle Book

Peter Pan

Beauty and the Beast

Aladdin

The Muppet Movie (original version)

The Muppets Take Manhattan

The Little Mermaid

Heidi's Song: Johanna Spyri's children's classic book *Heidi* retold in an animated musical movie with sixteen songs

Lady and the Tramp: an animated Disney classic with memorable songs

Just saying no and restricting our children's entertainment is not enough. Our ultimate goal is to help them learn to discern. Bob DeMoss, a former Focus on the Family youth culture specialist, says it's never too early to start teaching children to think critically about all forms of media, including music. "In fact, the earlier you activate the process," DeMoss says, "the better. Don't laugh. Beginning to teach four-year-olds how to think critically will help prevent them from becoming traditional American couch potatoes!"

DeMoss doesn't offer you a "just add water, mix, and microwave" recipe for the challenges facing you regarding music and entertainment, but in *Learn to Discern* he gives concrete steps you can take to get and keep your family on track and help your children develop discernment and critical thinking ability about music, television, and movies.

Resources to Help Parents Equip Children to Be Discerning About Music and Entertainment

Learn to Discern: Help for a Generation at Risk, featuring Bob DeMoss. A one-hundred-minute video that helps parents equip children and teens to think critically about music, movies, and television (produced by and available from Focus on the Family: 1-800-A-FAMILY).

Plugged In, a monthly magazine for parents of teens and preteens about current media, music, and movies. Call 800-A-FAMILY. Also available on their Web site, www.family.org/pplace/pi. You'll also find "Culture Clips" on the family.org Web site.

Mind over Media, by Stan Campbell and Randy Southern. A video and book for parents to guide their children in being discerning about music and entertainment. Available from Focus on the Family.

Audiocassettes: "What Should I Do If My Child Listens to Rock Music?" an informative message that gives down-to-earth yet biblical help for Christian parents who want to make wise decisions concerning rock music, and "Today's Music: A Window to Your Child's Soul," Al Menconi's seminar for parents that helps them understand the music culture of today's young people. (1-800-78-MUSIC)

Many videos of classical music performances are available from larger chains of video stores and from public libraries.

Music and Early Childhood, produced by First Steps in Music, Inc. This thirty-minute documentary gives parents and educators information about musical child development from birth through the early elementary years. Featuring the work of John Feierabend and the Connecticut Center for Early Childhood Education and Music and Movement.

Ballet on Video: Among others are *The Little Humpbacked Horse,* produced by Bolshoi Ballet Production, *Cinderella Ballet,* by Berlin Comic Opera, and *L'enfant et les sortilèges,* produced by Nederlands Dans Theater. These stories are told through ballet and are especially accessible and entertaining to children. Available through the catalog *Music for Little People* (800-727-2233) or from video stores and public libraries.

Music on Video, published by Films for the Humanities and Sciences, P.O. Box 2053, Princeton, NJ 08643-2053 (800-257-5126 or 609-452-1128). A wide variety of excellent music videos on the lives of composers, musical instruments, performances, history, and technology in music. On the expensive side but worth viewing. Call for a brochure, and see if perhaps your library will order it for you.

The Orchestra, by Mark Rubin and Alan Daniel. Book and tape read by Peter Ustinov and performed by the Toronto Philharmonic Orchestra. A great introduction to the instruments of the orchestra.

Check your local Christian bookstore for listings of videos from Christian production companies. Dramas and music videos are available.

Amazing Grace, available from Christian bookstores or Provident Bookstores, 616 Walnut Avenue, Scottsdale, PA 15683-1999 (412-887-8500). Documentary that shares the story behind the hymn "Amazing Grace." This remarkable video explores the song's history through the people who have sung it.

Hollywood Film Classics such as *Doctor Dolittle, Annie, Peter Pan, The Sound of Music, Mary Poppins, The Wizard of Oz, The Red Balloon, Heidi,* and *Rebecca of Sunnybrook Farm* are available and contain many of the wonderful songs such as "Over the Rainbow," "Do-Re-Mi," and "Tomorrow."

Mother Goose Goes to School, produced by Brentwood Kids Company, Brentwood Music. An exciting adventure for preschoolers. Sing-along songs about starting the day, science and discovery, the wonder of God's world, and the fun of learning.

Tiny Tot Pwaise, from Benson Music Group. This is among the first video series specifically designed for toddlers. Children ages one to four will be delighted with Arky the Ark and his friends. Arky represents safe biblical and wholesome values for families with small children. The videos feature electronic animation and live-action sequences with toddlers, places, and animals.

Wee Sing Videos, published by Price, Stern, and Sloan. (Wee Sing products are available in children's bookstores, music stores, and general and Christian bookstores.) This immensely popular series has sold millions of records and tapes. Full of favorite songs and rhymes, these sparkling bright one-hour videos capture a child's imagination. Songbook included. Titles include *Marvelous Musical Mansion, Wee Sing Together, Wee Sing in Sillyville,* and *Grandpa's Magical Toys.*

Chapter Nine

Music in Our
Spiritual Lives

God is its author; and not man;
He laid the keynote of all harmonies;
He planned all perfect combinations,
And He made us so that we could
Hear and understand.

ANONYMOUS

Hymns have been a distinguishing feature of Christianity for the past few centuries and especially during the last two hundred years. Often the sole representation of Christian faith in a movie or television program is the singing of a hymn. Songs of faith have softened the hearts of old sinners when regular arguments would do little good. Something about the combination of spirituality with music makes truth more palatable to some people, perhaps because music reaches us at more than various levels—conscious and subconscious, intuitive as well as cognitive. Music speaks to us in our spirits. In the story of David and Saul (1 Samuel 16:14-23), we see that music calmed Saul when he was tormented by an evil spirit; some Christians today claim that music can aid in spiritual deliverance. All of us are aware that something happens in us—spiritually, emotionally, mentally, and even physically—when God's truth and love minister to us in musical form.

Today we have more than hymns to give us musical food of the spirit.

Other styles of music make up our faith traditions and aid us as we learn, celebrate, meditate, and worship.

PURITAN PSALM SINGING

Although traditionally Puritans have not been viewed as giving music the place of prominence that other Christian traditions do, they actually felt music was a good gift of God, and they cherished music as an art. Many Puritans were able musicians and composers. They believed music's highest and best use was as an aid to worship.[1] They disdained what they considered to be the abuse of music—whether that meant singing bawdy, barroom songs or playing instruments in church.

The Puritans frowned on instrumental music in church because it lacked simplicity, but in their private homes, playing musical instruments was acceptable to entertain dinner guests or provide entertainment at a wedding reception.[2]

Psalters and Psalm books began to appear in the 1700s and contained a collection of the tunes most frequently sung. The introduction of one such book, *Bay Psalm Book,* describes the contents and their intended purpose: "The Psalms, Hymns, and Spiritual Songs, of the Old and New Testament… For the use, Edification, and Comfort of the Saints in publick and private, especially in New England. The Ninth Edition. Boston, 1698."[3]

SPIRITUALS

"As long as there have been slaves in this country, there have been spirituals," says Dr. Terry Terry, director of print music at Word, Inc., and a specialist in hymnology and musicology. Spirituals are religious songs of African-American origin with easily remembered choruses and repetitive verses. Often the leader sings a line or two and then the chorus or group sings the refrain.

Spirituals were passed down in the oral tradition, but not until the Civil War were they written down and collected. Although some melodies were said to originate in Africa, spirituals were also influenced by evangelistic preaching, revivals, and camp meetings in the South. Spiritual singing accompanied plantation labor, ship loading, and other work done by the African slaves.

Many spirituals were based on Bible characters and stories, and they reflect the faith, great emotion, suffering, and hope of the people. The spirituals sang much about heaven, and some reflected the Africans' view of themselves as modern children of Israel who hoped for deliverance from their bondage. Songs such as "Swing Low, Sweet Chariot," "Go Down, Moses," and "Climb Jacob's Ladder" are famous spirituals. Spirituals blossomed into gospel songs through the camp meeting and revival movements in America. We can also detect the spiritual's influence on rhythm and blues and jazz.

GOSPEL MUSIC

Gospel songs deal with personal religious experience, testimony, and exhortation. According to Dr. Terry, they are "me and my testimony and my need" songs, like "I Need Thee Every Hour," versus "We Worship the King" type hymns. Another example would be "Blessed Assurance, Jesus Is Mine," which is known as a gospel hymn. Hymns are more corporate—Christians as a body petitioning God or praising him together—whereas gospel music is more subjective, concerning a Christian's individual relationship with Jesus.

Gospel music is also harmonically slow and has a more simple chord structure than hymns. For example, if you're singing in A-flat, the chord structure under it is A-flat; in a hymn the chord structure changes with almost every beat. "This is part of the appeal of gospel music; it appeals more to the heart, and is not as intellectually taxing as a hymn," says Dr. Terry. Gospel songs were forerunners of contemporary praise-and-worship choruses. Since America's Bible Belt overlaps in many places with the South, there are some similarities between gospel music and country and Western, for example, simpler structure, personal lyrics, and similar rhythms.

CHORUSES FOR CONTEMPORARY PRAISE AND WORSHIP

These songs have a short, simple form and are learned easily by ear. "Father, I Adore You" is a good example of this musical style. Like "Seek Ye First," a chorus is often based on Scripture and is more personal than a hymn. "Contemporary choruses tend, like gospel songs, to be 'God and me songs,'" says Bill Wolaver, music composer and founder of WriteSong Resources. The tempo of choruses varies; some are quite lively and joyful, while others are slow, like a prayer the person is singing, speaking to God rather than just describing God.

Praise and worship songs from publishers Vineyard Praise, Hosanna Integrity, Shepherd's Heart, and Hillsongs are combinations of choruses and contemporary worship songs. They include popular styles and rock beats, orchestra sections, and rhythm sections. They feature guitars, keyboards, drums, and even acoustic instruments, as opposed to the organ and piano of traditional church music. This is a broad category that includes some more meditative and quietly worshipful songs and others full of celebration like "Shout to the Lord" or militant banner songs like "Lift High the Banner of Love."

Christian contemporary music appeals to young people and to the commercial ear, which enables it to compete with secular stations, says Dr. Terry. Much of children's Christian music is more contemporary material for kids and has a pop sound. Influenced by public television's *Sesame Street* and other programs, it tends to be lighter in nature, having very few acoustic instruments, and mainly uses synthesizers. Like the Psalty series of children's music, much of it is either Scripture set to music or songs that teach honesty, obedience to God and parents, and other biblical values.

Although some might consider the contemporary praise music too untraditional and secular, such disagreements are not new. Even in the 1700s conflict between traditional church singing and the "free style of the folk" arose! Conservatives wanted to keep singing Wesleyan hymns exactly the way they had been sung, but people preferred the lively revival hymns and popular spiritual songs that sprang up in the camp meetings after 1799.[4]

The author of "Amazing Grace," John Newton, was considered to be rebellious in his music, and his hymns were criticized as being too emotionally expressive.[5] But now we view hymns such as this one as traditional—and quite tame by modern standards.

HYMNS

Hymns are songs designed to praise and honor God. A strong part of our American spiritual heritage, hymns are still sung in many churches across the United States. Considered traditional church music, they express religious devotion, praise and thanks to God, or instruction and are set to singable tunes that repeat for successive stanzas. They were part of evangelical movements and revivals through history, such as the Great Awakening of 1734–70. Modern hymnals contain choice hymns from the past as well as more contemporary worship songs.

Some of the most prominent hymn authors are Martin Luther (1483–1546), Isaac Watts (1674–1748), Charles Wesley (1707–88), John Newton (1725–1807), and Fanny Crosby (1820–1915).

As Al Menconi, youth music specialist, says, "Beautiful hymns are often overlooked in our rush for the new and unique. I believe Christians of all ages and musical tastes should learn to appreciate the quality and depth of the hymns of our spiritual heritage."[6] Hymns require a little more effort to learn than some of the popular choruses, but the effort is certainly worthwhile.

The hymns and hymn stories that follow are just a small sampling of the wonderful hymns of our faith. Even if your church does not sing hymns, you can learn some and teach them to your children (see below for suggestions), perhaps learning a "Hymn of the Month."

An excellent way to familiarize yourself with hymns is to consult a companion book to your favorite hymnal; another is to buy a DaySpring calendar with the hymn theme (each day a hymn is featured with some interesting stories and facts); another is to consult some of the books at the end of this chapter that contain hymn stories. You will find hymns to be a comfort during hard times, a challenge to live out great Christian principles, a source of strength, and an inspiration.

Introducing Hymns to Your Children

- If you know a hymn is going to be sung on a special occasion at church, teach it to your child first at home. Then when it is sung at church, he will enjoy it even more because the tune will be familiar. One mother wrote out a simplified version of "Christ the Lord Is Risen Today" and taught it to her six-year-old son. She played it on the piano, and they sang it together. "He lit up when we sang it as a congregation on Easter Sunday and he could join right in!" she said.

- Choose a "Hymn of the Month" to learn and practice singing together as a family. Share the hymn's background information (including the Scripture reference, if it originates from one) before you teach it to your child. Many hymns have an interesting history behind their writing. (See the information about many famous hymns and the recommended books of hymn stories in the following list.)

- Purchase a hymnal to have at home. They are available at book fairs, used-book stores, or Christian bookstores. Sometimes churches sell or give away old hymnals when they get updated ones.

- When introducing a hymn, sing it several times to your child. Play the tune on an instrument if possible. If your child plays an instrument, encourage him or her to try to play the tune.

- Find a collection of favorite hymns on CD and play them at home or in the car.

If you include hymns in the variety of musical styles your family listens to, hymns will be more enjoyable. In the Lough family, Posy and Tom have always played hymns on the piano, so their son Kyser has grown up with them. On Sunday mornings, the one who gets dressed first for church gets to play the piano—a good way to set a cheerful tone in the house at a time that is often harried!

Wee Sing Bible Songs and *Wee Sing Christmas Songs* are good tools for introducing simple hymns and Christmas hymns to young children. They come with cassette tapes and music books that contain words and piano and guitar chord symbols for playing and singing at home.

Some Hymns to Learn and Enjoy and the Stories Behind Them

"Amazing Grace" (NEW BRITAIN) C.M.

The tune to "Amazing Grace" is an American folk melody that originally appeared anonymously in *Virginia Harmony* in 1831. E. O. Excell's arrangement of that melody, which first appeared in *Make His Praise Glorious* in 1900, has been widely accepted.

The words to "Amazing Grace" were written by John Newton, based on 2 Corinthians 9:8, and first appeared in 1779. Newton was the captain of a slave ship before his conversion to Christ, and then he became an English evangelist. This hymn is much better known in America than in his native England and has been used extensively in churches, concert halls, radio, and television.

"Blessed Be the Tie That Binds" S.M.

John Fawcett pastored a small village church in Yorkshire, England, where he had served faithfully for seven years with barely enough income to support his growing family. John received an invitation to pastor a new and much larger church in London, at a much higher salary. Excited by the prospect of a new ministry, he accepted the call and announced his decision to his congregation. It was a difficult announcement because he and his wife had developed a deep love for their congregation.

On the day of their parting, wagons loaded and the tearful people of their church surrounding them to say good-bye, John's wife said, "I know not how to bear this or how to go!" "Nor I," replied John. "Nor will we go. Unload the wagons and put everything back."

John pastored there until he died fifty-four years later, and today he is best remembered not for the books, sermons, or essays he wrote, but for the simple hymn that reflects his and his wife's inability to part with their beloved church. The music was composed by Johann Naegeli.

"A Mighty Fortress Is Our God" (EIN' FESTE BURG) 8.7.8.7.6.6.6.6.7. This sturdy, mighty hymn, a paraphrase of Psalm 46, was written by Martin Luther in 1529 and is among the thirty-seven hymns that he wrote. The translation is by Frederick Hedge, and the hymn is most often used on Reformation Sunday in Protestant churches all over the world. The hymn dates from 1529 and is thought to have been written at the time of the Diet of Speyer, when the German princes made a formal protest against the attacks on their liberties and hence gained the name "Protestants." The tune is also attributed to Luther and has been used by later composers in some of their compositions

---

Hymns Are Identified By:

Hymn names—usually the first words of the first stanza (called the incipit)

Text author's name—which appears under the title on the left

Composer's name—which appears under the title on the right

Title of tune or melody—which appears just beneath text title or at the bottom of the page. For example, tune to "Amazing Grace" is called NEW BRITAIN.

Meter—the number of lines in a stanza and number of syllables in the line. Example: There are seven syllables in "Jesus loves me, this I know" in each line, so the meter is 7.7.7.7. The major meters are
C.M. (Common Meter) 8.6.8.6
S.M. (Short Meter) 6.6.8.6.
L.M. (Long Meter) 8.8.8.8

(Mendelssohn: Reformation Symphony, fifth movement; Bach: Cantata No. 80; Wagner: Kaisermarsch).

"Blessed Assurance" (ASSURANCE) 9.10.9.9. with Refrain
The words for this hymn were written by Fanny Crosby, the most prolific of gospel hymn writers. Blind from infancy, she wrote over eight thousand hymns before her death at age ninety-five. She lived a radiant life and expressed her joy and hope in Christ through her hymn writing.

Many of her hymns were written spontaneously. One day Phoebe Palmer Knapp played a melody on the piano for Fanny and asked if it suggested any words to her. Crosby replied, "Why, the music says, 'blessed assurance, Jesus is mine.'" Shortly afterward, she handed her friend the completed lyrics to the song, based on James 5:13.

This hymn is considered to be Fanny Crosby's best. It first appeared in *Gems of Praise* in 1873 and became a very popular hymn in America and England.

"Jesus Loves Me" (JESUS LOVES ME) 7.7.7.7. with Refrain
The most famous of all children's (and even adults') hymns in the world was composed by William Batchelder Bradbury in 1861. The words were written by Anna Bartlett Warner, who also wrote under the pen name "Amy Lothrop." She included "Jesus Loves Me" in her religious novel *Say and Seal*. In the story, one of the characters was taught the song by his Sunday school teacher. Warner wrote, "For the time being Johnny Fax was so intensely real, so vividly in my heart, that the hymn was written for him as if he had been a living child."

Although the song is simple, theologians such as Francis Schaeffer have said that "Jesus Loves Me" conveys a certainty of biblical truth that leads to peace and freedom for people all over the world. Missionaries have reported it as a favorite hymn of the children of China and other countries, and it is an effective way to explain the gospel in a clear and simple way to those of different languages.

"It Is Well with My Soul" (VILLE DU HAVRE) 11.8.11.9. with refrain
The tune for this hymn was composed by Philip Bliss and was published first in *Gospel Hymns No. 2* in 1876. The text was written by a successful American attorney, Horatio Gates Spafford. On the advice of his doctor and to benefit his wife's health, he scheduled a trip to England for himself, his wife, and four of their daughters. Due to unexpected business developments, he was unable to accompany them, so the family went without him.

During the crossing, their ship, the SS *Ville du Havre,* collided with another ship and sank quickly. Spafford's wife was saved, but the children died. She was taken to Cardiff, Wales, with the other survivors where she cabled her husband the message: "Saved alone." Spafford shortly thereafter, while on board another ship, wrote the words to "It Is Well with My Soul," close to the scene of the tragedy. The Scripture reference is Job 1:21.

"Silent Night" (STILLE NACHT) Irregular
On December 24, 1818, in the little village of Oberndorf, Austria, the organ would not work, and the Christmas Eve music could not be played for the special Christmas service. Father Joseph Mohr, a priest, wrote the words to a new song and asked the organist, Franz Gruber, to compose the tune. That evening, "Silent Night," written for two voices and a guitar, was sung in the Christmas Eve service. It is perhaps the most popular Christmas hymn throughout Europe and the Americas. The Scripture reference is Luke 2:16.

"Just As I Am" (WOODWORTH) L.M.
This has been called the world's greatest soul-winning hymn. It was written in 1834 and first published in *The Invalid's Hymn Book* in 1836 in six four-line stanzas. The author, Charlotte Elliot, wrote the hymn after being awake all night, distressed about her constant illness and her inability to help prepare for a church bazaar that would raise money for a school for underprivileged children. Too weak to go to the bazaar with her family and friends, she felt discouraged that she could do nothing to serve God. In this turmoil and physical suffering, she wrote the words to the poem for her own comfort and for the strengthening of her faith, based on John 6:37: "Whoever comes to me I will never drive away."[7]

The song quickly became an inspiration to many others in England, America, and all over the world. D. L. Moody said that this invalid's hymn drew as many people to Christ as the sermons he preached at his hundreds of evangelistic services. Billy Graham has used the hymn in crusades on every continent. The tune was written by William Bradbury and first included in the *Mendelssohn Collection* in 1849.[8]

"Christ the Lord Is Risen Today" (EASTER HYMN) 7.7.7.7.
Charles Wesley wrote the text of this great hymn of the resurrection of Christ based on 1 Corinthians 15:20. The tune to this hymn is also called WOR-GAN and is anonymous, first appearing in *Lyra Davidica* in 1708. The present

form of this hymn was published in 1740 in John Wesley's *Foundery Collection*. Originally the "alleluias" were not included at the end of each line, but they were added later when the hymn was adapted to the tune EASTER HYMN.

"Holy, Holy, Holy! Lord God Almighty!" (NICAEA) 11.12.12.10
This hymn of adoration and worship is included in most English hymnals and has been translated into many other languages. It was originally written to be sung on Trinity Sunday, eight weeks after Easter, and was first published in 1826. It is a paraphrase of Revelation 4:8-11 and was written by Reginald Heber while he was a vicar in Shropshire, England.

The tune, NICAEA, was composed by John Dykes to accompany Heber's hymn and was first published with the text in 1861. The tune name is drawn from the theme of the hymn, but also from the fact that the doctrine of the Trinity was established as an accepted doctrine at an ecumenical council held at Nicaea in A.D. 325.

"How Great Thou Art" (O STORE GUD) 11.10.11.10. with Refrain
This hymn was sung in other parts of the world before being introduced to North America by George Beverly Shea and Cliff Barrows at the Toronto Billy Graham Crusade in 1955. It first came to their attention in 1954 in London when a publisher showed it to them.

The hymn originated in Sweden and was written by Carl Boberg, who is said to have been inspired by the beauty of the Swedish lakes during a thunderstorm. It was translated into German and then Russian, where it became a very popular evangelical hymn. Missionaries to Russia, the Reverend and Mrs. Stewart Hine, became acquainted with the hymn there and introduced it to many friends. At the end of World War II, Reverend Hine wrote a fourth stanza that was included in a 1949 English publication by Hine. The Billy Graham Evangelistic Association has used the hymn many times in their crusades since 1955. The Scripture reference is Psalm 48:1.

Some of the information in this chapter was adapted from the following books. They are excellent resources for further study of the fascinating stories behind our favorite hymns.

Billy Graham Team. *Crusade Hymns and Hymn Stories.* Chicago: Hope Publishing, 1967.

Buche, Emory Stevens, ed. *Companion to the Hymnal* (Methodist). Nashville: Abingdon, 1970.

Haeussler, Armin. *The Story of Our Hymns* (Evangelical and Reformed Church). St. Louis: Eden Publishing, 1952.

Reynolds, William Jensen. *Hymns of Our Faith* (Baptist). Nashville: Broadman Press, 1964.

Reynolds, William Jensen, and Milburn Price. *A Joyful Sound.* 2d ed. (General Hymnody) New York: Holt, Rinehart & Winston, 1978.

Schoenhals, Lawrence R., ed. *Companion to Hymns of Faith and Life* (Free Methodist). Winona Lake, Ind.: Light and Life Press; and Marion, Ind.: The Wesley Press, 1980.

Smith, Jane Stuart, and Betty Carlson. *Favorite Women Hymn Writers.* Wheaton, Ill.: Crossway, 1990.

Chapter Ten

Classics Month-by-Month

*The trouble with music appreciation in general
is that people are taught to have too much respect for music;
they should be taught to love it instead.*

IGOR STRAVINSKY

Classics Month-by-Month" is a full year of classical music enjoyment and instruction for families and homeschooling parents who want their kids to get the benefit of classical music. It is also for teachers from preschool or kindergarten level up who want to bring classical music into the classroom. Whether you know much about classical music or not, you can enjoy this chapter and introduce some wonderful music to your child. Resources are included that help children learn about and appreciate classical music—such as the Classical Kids CDs and videos. For example, one of these, *Beethoven Lives Upstairs,* uses a delightful story form to describe Beethoven's life and how he created his music and includes selections of his best music. It has recently been made into a film that is available in video.

Time has a way of sifting the worthy from the unworthy, the lasting from the transient. Time will remember the best composers and compositions of our time, just as it has remembered those of the past. Classical music has survived the test of time because of its ability to create memories of past eras, and yet we can relate to it today. It's never too early to enjoy this music, nor is it ever too late. It does require some effort, but once the effort has been made, the rewards are there!

Classical music has the potential to challenge and to open new experiences to its listeners: experiences that go deep, that are lasting, that enrich, that elevate, that educate. All that is necessary is for the listener to have an open mind.

"Classics Month-by-Month" is designed for those with little or no experience and for those who have experience and need a springboard to begin helping their children appreciate and learn about classical music. In each month of this chapter you will find:

- a brief biography of a composer
- a composition of that composer selected with children in mind
- suggested resources related to that composer
- a list of vocabulary words with definitions
- a suggested activity
- a brief quiz that could be used as a summary of the chapter or as an element in homeschool curriculum

In addition to the material found in this chapter, please note that a "Time Line of Selected Composers" immediately follows the chapter. This will give you the big picture of the different musical styles and composers, along with their birthdays. With this resource you could celebrate a composer's birthday each month. "A Parent's and Teacher's Guide to Music Resources," appendix B, will give many suggestions for audiocassettes, CDs, records, books, videos, and other helpful tools, with leads for finding more information.

My special thanks again to Marilyn Rosfeld, DMA and adjunct professor, Oklahoma City University, for her contributions and knowledge of composers, their music, their place in history, and other technical information in this section.

COMPOSERS AND COMPOSITIONS

In the past three hundred to five hundred years, many gifted composers have created numerous works in a great variety of styles. Choosing a limited number of composers for this section was difficult. Different works are important to different people. Many of the musical compositions suggested are here not only because they are classical but because they appeal to young listeners. But many other composers not listed here (Claude Debussy, Richard Strauss, Igor Stravinsky) are well worth learning about. One of the best sources is Stanley Sadie's *Brief Guide to Music,* 2d ed. (Prentice Hall, 1987), which has a basic guide, seven records, audiocassettes, or CDs, a ninety-minute student cassette, listening helps, and other resources.

The composers are arranged in chronological order, but you can change the order without adversely affecting the content. For instance, Handel's *Messiah* may be studied in the Christmas season, or Bach's passion music saved for

Easter. You can adapt games from chapter 6, "Music Games and Activities," to go along with the one suggested for each month. Here are some words to be familiar with before beginning your classics journey:

accent	emphasis on a specific note or chord
beat	unit used to measure musical time
chord	a combination of musical tones sounded together
harmony	the relationship of pitches sounded simultaneously
instrumental	classification of instruments according to timbre into sections: string, woodwind, brass, and percussion
interval	the distance between any two pitches
measure (bar)	a consistent time unit within a composition indicated by vertical lines through a staff
melody	a single-line succession of pitches making up a meaningful whole
meter	the arrangements of beats in measures with regular recurring accents
pitch	highness or lowness of a musical tone
range	the entire series of notes from low to high that a voice or instrument is capable of performing
rhythm	duration or length of pitches
staff	five horizontal lines and spaces upon which musical pitches are placed
syncopation	shifting of accents to unexpected beats
tempo	rate of speed
texture	the relationships among the various notes in a composition, both as they sound together (vertically) and as they follow one another (horizontally)
timbre	color, or quality of sound
tune	a kind of melody that can readily be sung
vocal	classification of voices according to range and timbre from high to low: soprano, mezzo soprano, alto, tenor, baritone, bass
Western music	refers mainly to the classical music of Europe and the Americas (also called "Western art music")

MONTH 1

Antonio Vivaldi (March 4, 1678–July 28, 1741)

Vivaldi was born in Italy in 1678. He was the son of a violinist, was ordained into the Catholic church in his twenties, and came to be known as the "red priest," probably because of his red hair. He was *maestro de concerti* at the four most important music schools in Venice. One of these institutions, the Pio Ospedale della Pietà (for orphaned girls), was reputed to have one of the finest orchestras in all of Italy. Judging from the music Vivaldi wrote for these girls, they were expert performers. Vivaldi spent time in other Italian cities and in Amsterdam. He died in Vienna in 1741 and was buried in a pauper's grave.

In Vivaldi's time there was constant public demand for new music. There were no classics to depend on, and few compositions of any kind survived more than two or three seasons. Vivaldi was expected to furnish new oratorios and concertos for every festival at the Pietà. During his lifetime, he wrote prolifically, accumulating some five hundred concertos, forty-nine operas, ninety solo and trio sonatas, and many cantatas, oratorios, and motets. Vivaldi was able to compose with phenomenal speed and prided himself on being able to compose a concerto faster than a copyist could copy the parts. His influence on future generations included his style of writing for the string orchestra, the role of the soloist in instrumental works, clarity of form, and logical continuity of musical ideas.

Suggested Compositions

The Four Seasons. This set of four violin concertos is probably Vivaldi's best known composition. Each concerto is titled with one of the four seasons: *Spring (La Primavera), Summer (L'estate), Autumn (L'autunno),* and *Winter (L'inverno).* The music describes the composer's reaction to the seasons. Poems accompany each movement. Each line of the poem is printed above a certain passage in the music, and the music at that point mirrors as graphically as possible the action described. Actions such as "the singing of birds," "lightning and thunder," "baying of dogs," "teeth chattering from the cold," and "people slipping on the ice" occur during their respective pieces.

Violin Concerto in A Minor, Op. 3, No. 6. Vivaldi wrote nearly five hundred concertos, two hundred of which were for the violin. This concerto is from among the first twelve published and was titled *L'estro armonico,* meaning "musical fancy." It has three movements—fast, slow, fast—and in addition to solo violin, it uses first and second violins, viola, cello, violone, and continuo.

Related Materials

Vivaldi's Ring of Mystery (audiocassette no. 8235 by Sue Hammond). The story revolves around a child who enters Vivaldi's life while he is the music director at an orphanage in Venice. Katrina is curious about her origins, and with the help of Giovanni, the gondolier, and Vivaldi, she finds her answer. There are over two dozen examples of Vivaldi's music, including the *Four Seasons*.

Trio Sonata Op. 3, No. 2, by **Arcangelo Corelli** (1653–1713). These trio sonatas were the crowning achievement of Italian chamber music in the late 1600s. His sonatas and concertos used techniques that were followed for the next fifty years. This sonata has four movements: slow, fast, slow, fast. It is scored for two violins, one viola, and one continuo part (cello and keyboard).

Christmas Concerto Op. 6, No. 8, by Corelli. Concertos were often played in church as overtures before or at some point during Mass. Many composers of the time composed an optional pastoral movement to be used with the Christmas Mass. Corelli's *Christmas Concerto* contains one of the most beautiful and best known pastorals.

Trumpet Sonata in D. This sonata by **Henry Purcell** (1659–95) actually resembles a concerto since it is scored for trumpet and chamber orchestra. Its three movements follow the fast-slow-fast tempo scheme favored during the late seventeenth century. This work is representative of Purcell's instrumental composition.

Vocabulary

cantata	a composition for voices (solo and chorus) accompanied by instruments and having several movements; like an oratorio but shorter and not always on a religious topic
concerto	a composition of three or more movements (sections fast, slow, fast—written for a solo instrument (piano, violin, clarinet, etc.) and orchestra
concerto grosso	an instrumental composition in which a small group of solo instruments, called a concertino, alternates with the full orchestra, called the tutti or *ripieno*
continuo (basso continuo)	an accompaniment played on a keyboard instrument, usually harpsichord or organ, assisted by a bass melody instrument—cello, viola da gamba, or bassoon—usually improvised from a bass line with numbers indicating chords (figured bass)
form	musical structure; the way the elements (pitch, melody, harmony, rhythm) of a musical composition are put together
motet	a composition for singers without instrumental accompaniment, dating from the thirteenth century, usually with Latin texts and having sacred subjects

movement   a major section in a long instrumental work (sonata, concerto), able to stand alone but related to the other movements (sections) of a composition by key, tempo, thematic content, etc.

opera   a play with characters and scenery in which the characters usually sing their parts and are usually accompanied by an orchestra

operetta   similar to but shorter than an opera

opus (Op.)   a term used to catalog a composer's works, usually in chronological order (opus 1 = first work); an opus may contain several pieces designated by the term "number"; thus an opus 6 may contain numbers 1, 2, 3, etc.

oratorio   a musical composition most often based on a biblical subject, for soloists, chorus, and orchestra; somewhat like an opera but without the staging

sonata   a piece for solo instrument(s) in three movements that are usually fast, slow, fast

trio sonata a piece for two solo instruments and continuo in three movements that are usually fast, slow, fast

Suggested Activity: Meter Detection

Purpose: To hear the difference between songs with 3 and 4 beats per measure.

Although there are many different meters, from simple to complex, most of the common songs and hymns we sing are in 3/4 and 4/4 meters. Learning to detect differences in meter develops an understanding of basic rhythmic structure in music. For this activity we focus on songs with 3 and 4 beats per measure.

Sing and/or play songs in these meters, and listen for the places of stress. These stressed or accented notes will be beat one. Try to count to either three or four very steadily, and see which fits the music before the next stressed beat occurs.

Below are a few examples. Please note that some syllables receive more than one beat ("Old MacDonald") or less than one beat ("Lavender's Blue"), and that some normally stressed beats have no syllable ("Sound of Music").

Examples with 4 beats per measure:
Twin-kle, twin-kle **lit**-tle star **How** I won-der
1   2   3   4   1 2 3 4 1   2 3   4
Old Mac-Don-ald **had** a farm **ee** i ee i **oh**
1   2   3   4   1 2 3 4   1   2 3   4 1 2 3

Go tell Aunt **Rho** -die, **Go** tell Aunt **Rho** - o - die
1 2 3 4   12   3 4 12 3 4   1   2 3 4

Examples with 3 beats per measure:
Lav-en-der's **blue** dil-ly dil-ly **lav**-en-der's **green**
1   2   3   1   2   3   1   2 3   1 2 3
E   -del-**weiss**, **e**   -del-**weiss**
1 2 3   1 2 3 12 3   1 2 3

Some pieces begin with a nonstressed syllable or "pick-up" note.
Example with 4 beats per measure:
The **hills** are a-live   with the sound of   **mu**-sic
4   1   2   3 4 1 2   3   4 1 2 3 4

Example with 3 beats per measure:
Hap-py **birth**-day to **you** hap-py **birth**-day to **you** hap-py
3   1   2   3 1 2 3   1   2 3 1 2 3

Look through any songbook or hymnal and find other familiar songs.
After you become proficient in detecting 3/4 and 4/4 meter, try other meters.
Learn also to detect the meter of the music you hear or sing.

Quiz

I. Fill in the blanks with the correct words:
_____ 1. musical structure
_____ 2. a composition for chorus, soloists, and orchestra with a biblical
subject
_____ 3. a composition written for a solo instrument and orchestra in three
movements
_____ 4. a term used to help catalog a composer's works
_____ 5. a piece for a solo instrument in three movements

II. True/false
_____ 1. Vivaldi wrote a piece called the "Four Seasonings" about salt, pep-
per, chili, and oregano.
_____ 2. Vivaldi wrote very slowly and consequently wrote a small amount
of music.
_____ 3. Vivaldi was a teacher in a music school that was associated with an
institution for orphaned girls.

MONTH 2

Johann Sebastian Bach
(March 21, 1685–July 28, 1750)

J. S. Bach was born in the central German town of Eisenach in 1685 (same birth year as Handel and Scarlatti) into a family with a tradition of composers, singers, and instrumentalists. Bach had a total of twenty children, but only half survived infancy. His first wife, Maria Barbara, died in 1720 (seven children), and he later married Anna Magdalena (thirteen children). Four of Bach's children followed musical careers (Wilhelm Friedemann, Carl Philipp Emanuel, Johann Christoph, and Johann Christian).

Bach held three important posts during his long career: organist in the town of Weimar, 1708–17; director of music for the prince of Cöthen, 1717–23; and cantor of the church of Saint Thomas in Leipzig, from 1723 until his death in 1750.

His position in history is that of one who developed existing forms rather than created new ones. He meshed the three great national traditions of his time—German, Italian, and French—into a unity never before equaled. His mastery of the techniques of composition is unparalleled.

Bach was a very religious man. He felt that "the aim and final reason of all music should be nothing else but the Glory of God and the refreshment of the spirit." He inscribed "To God alone be the praise" at the end of all of his religious works. He established the German Lutheran chorales or hymns that became a strong statement of faith.

He was also an excellent organist and composed many works for organ. When complimented on his playing, he commented, "There is nothing remarkable about it. All you have to do is hit the right notes at the right time and the instrument plays itself."

He also wrote a lot of music for the harpsichord and clavichord, including his *Well-Tempered Clavier,* consisting of forty-eight preludes and fugues in two volumes, "French" and "English" suites, partitas, "Chromatic Fantasy and Fugue," *Italian Concerto, Goldberg Variations,* and others. He also wrote teaching pieces for his children and for his wife, Anna Magdalena. Some of these pieces are included in a collection called the *Little Clavier Book of Anna Magdalena Bach.* These pieces and others ("inventions," "sinfonias," *Little Clavier Book of W. Friedemann Bach,* etc.) are played today by students studying the piano. Even though Bach wrote these works with the harpsichord and clavichord in mind, his works are played most often on the piano today. (The piano was invented in 1709 by Bartolomeo Cristofori and developed throughout the eighteenth century.)

Bach composed for various combinations of instruments, both small and large. Of special interest are his six *Brandenburg Concertos,* four suites for orchestra, and six sonatas for unaccompanied violin.

He also composed a great volume of choral music. He wrote over two hundred cantatas and the two "Passions" (according to Saint John and Saint Matthew), and his famous *B-Minor Mass.*

Besides his active life related to his church posts, he taught both musical and nonmusical subjects to choirboys, and was often called upon to test and inaugurate new organs. At one such occasion at the court of Frederick the Great at Potsdam, Bach offered to improvise on a theme given to him by the king. He improvised one of his astonishing fugues, and after returning to Leipzig further elaborated on it, added a trio sonata, and returned his new composition, "The Musical Offering," to the monarch.

Bach was interested in various numerology theories and used the spelling of his name B-A-C-H, which in German has musical significance, namely the pitches B-flat A C B. This interesting motif was first used in the last fugue of his *Art of the Fugue.* Since Bach's death, many other composers have used this motif as the basis of compositions.

During his later years Bach's eyesight failed him, and he eventually became blind. The sheer volume of work produced by this composer is unparalleled. But its high quality, consistency, and complexity are also unparalleled. Some sources have stated that Bach would have had to average twenty to twenty-one pages of manuscript every day of his adult life in order to complete the writing of all his compositions.

Suggested Compositions

"Organ Fugue in G Minor." This piece for organ is often called the "little" organ fugue to distinguish it from the "great" organ fugue, a more extensive work written later. This brilliant fugue has four voices, with the subject beginning in the upper voice, passing through the other voices, and concluding on the pedals. Another popular organ piece is the "Toccata and Fugue in D Minor."

Suite No. 3 in D Major. This piece is scored for two oboes, three trumpets, drums, first and second violins, violas, and basso continuo and consists of five movements: *Overture, Air, Gavotte, Bourrée,* and *Gigue.* The popular "Air for the G String" has been adapted from the second movement. The orchestral suites show a lighter side of Bach's composition.

Brandenburg Concerto No. 2. This is one of six small concertos written for the Margrave Christian Ludwig of Brandenburg. It contains three movements. It is in the concerto grosso style in which two instrumental groups vie with each other. The solo group (concertino) consists of trumpet, flute, oboe, and violin; the accompanying group (tutti) includes first and second violins, violas, and double basses. The continuo is played by cello or harpsichord.

"O Sacred Head, Now Wounded," hymn chorale

Related Materials

Mr. Bach Comes to Call (audiocassette 8186 by Sue Hammond). Eight-year-old Elizabeth is practicing Bach's "Minuet in G" when the composer appears with his magic orchestra and chair and tells of his life and music. Winner of the Notable Children's Recording Award, 1989 Juno award nomination for Best Children's Recording, and 1989 Parents' Choice Award. (Teacher's Guide available: 80M07861)

Vocabulary

aria
an elaborate solo song, generally with instrumental accompaniment, occurring in operas, cantatas, and oratorios

brass section
the part of the orchestra consisting of trumpets, French horns, trombones, tubas

BWV
a cataloging system used exclusively for Bach's works, abbreviation of Bach-Werke-Verzeichnis

chorus
in an oratorio or opera, a composition for a choir consisting of sopranos, altos, tenors, and basses and accompanied by an orchestra

clavichord
a rectangular box with a keyboard in which the strings are struck by metal tangents (small blades)

fugue
a composition in which two or more (usually three or four) voice parts state a subject (theme). In the beginning, one voice alone introduces the subject that is then imitated by other voices in close succession and reappears throughout the entire piece repeatedly in all the voices at different places. Statements of the subject alternate with episodes based on sequentially treated motifs drawn from the subject.

harpsichord	a keyboard instrument that resembles a piano, in which the strings are plucked
legato	a direction to perform smoothly, without breaks between the notes
organ	a keyboard instrument in which sound is produced by vibrating columns of air in various sized pipes
percussion section	the part of the orchestra consisting of instruments that are struck (drums, bells, etc.)
prelude	used as an introductory piece to liturgical services, or more commonly as an introduction to another composition, such as a fugue and suite
recitative	a short portion sung in a style that resembles speech, with little change in pitch, and flexible rhythm that follows the structure of the text
staccato	a direction to perform detached, with breaks between indicated notes
string section	the part of the orchestra made up of violins, violas, cellos, and basses. Each instrument consists basically of a body, neck, four strings, tuning pegs, and a bridge and is played with a bow or plucked.
suite	a collection of dance movements titled gigue, bourrée, air, gavotte, sarabande, minuet, etc.
woodwind section	the part of the orchestra consisting of piccolos, flutes, oboes, English horns, clarinets, and bassoons

Suggested Activity: Early Instrument Identification

Purpose: To learn to identify early instruments and see how instruments of today have developed from these early models.

Locate a book at your library that includes information about and pictures of seventeenth- and early eighteenth-century instruments (or even earlier). Choose three or four of your favorites, and find out all you can about them. Look in your area for a museum, university, or large church that might have some of these instruments. Attend a concert where some of these early instruments might be used. Check to see if there is a society for the preservation of early music in your area. Try to find a video that will feature these instruments and music composed for them. Look for recordings, audiocassettes, or CDs that feature early music played on early instruments.

Quiz

I. Draw lines to connect the instruments to the correct family:

violin, viola, cello, bass   brass family

drums, timpani, celeste, triangle   string family

flute, clarinet, oboe, bassoon   percussion family

trumpet, horn, trombone, tuba   woodwind family

II. True/false

_____ 1. Bach lived and died in California.

_____ 2. Bach had twenty children.

_____ 3. Bach wrote "To God alone be the praise" at the end of his religious compositions.

MONTH 3

George Frideric Handel (February 23, 1685–April 14, 1759)

Handel was born in Halle, Germany. His father, a surgeon, wanted him to become a lawyer. However, when his musical talent was discovered quite by accident by Duke Johann Adolph, plans were made for his musical career.

He moved to Hamburg, Germany, then went to Italy where he learned the craft of writing Italian operas. His dream was to move to London, and in his late twenties he did so. His first opera, *Rinaldo,* was presented in Italian for English-speaking audiences. It was a huge success. For a number of years, Handel enjoyed a generous stipend from the royal family and other patrons and the opportunity to pursue his composing career. He was able to start an opera company, the Royal Academy of Music, and as he composed, he recruited investors, engaged singers, and performed his administrative duties.

A movement away from Italian opera to English libretto texts in the 1720s led to a decline in Handel's career. He was criticized for being old-fashioned and lacking inspiration. He also suffered from an attack of palsy that limited the use of his right hand. Within time his health was restored, and he continued composing and performing, but without success. By 1741, he was heavily in debt.

A wealthy poet named Charles Jennens had been trying for years to interest Handel in setting some of his texts to music. One morning the text for *Messiah* arrived, and Handel decided to compose music for it. It was not about the Bible but was scripture from the Bible and consisted of prophecies and other scriptures about Christ, his birth, death, and resurrection. It was in the form of an oratorio. The lord lieutenant of Ireland invited Handel to Dublin to perform a work for charity, and Handel chose this work. Reviewers were very complimentary, and the performance was a success. With renewed inspiration, Handel continued to compose other oratorios, and each year during his last ten years, *Messiah* was offered for charity. Gradually, London audiences began to flock to performances, and when King George II heard it, he was most enthusiastic. When the "Hallelujah Chorus" was presented, he stood to his feet. It is still customary for the audience to stand during the singing of the "Hallelujah Chorus."

The success of *Messiah* renewed Handel's confidence and helped save him from obscurity. In spite of blindness, he continued to compose and perform until his death on April 14, 1759.

Suggested Compositions

Messiah. This piece is rarely heard today in its entirety because of its length. Usually at Christmas, portions including the overture, recitatives, arias, and choruses are presented, and occasionally a very small portion might be used in a church service at various times of the year. Other Handel oratorios based on the Bible include *Samson, Judas Maccabeus,* and *Israel in Egypt.*

Water Music. A suite written in 1717 for the royal procession of barges on the Thames. This suite contains more than twenty movements, with special importance given to the brass throughout. Happy, dancelike movements alternate and contrast with the joyful and powerful brass fanfares.

"Largo" from *Xerxes (Serse).* This famous operatic piece was originally an aria, but it has become even more famous through a variety of instrumental transcriptions.

"Joy to the World" and "Thine Be the Glory," hymns

Related Materials

Berreby, David. "The Man Who Wrote *Messiah.*" *Reader's Digest,* April 1992, 227-40.

Sonata in E Major, K. 46, by **Domenico Scarlatti** (1685–1757). Scarlatti wrote more than five hundred sonatas for the harpsichord, now played on the piano. These are one-movement compositions in two-part form. The *Sonata in E* is typical of many of the sonatas with its brilliant runs and scale passages, use of high and low register, trills, arpeggios, and abrupt contrasts of style.

"Solfegietto." This piece, written by **Carl Philipp Emanuel Bach** (1714-88), son of the famous J. S. Bach, is a favorite intermediate-level piece for piano and is included in many current piano literature books.

Vocabulary

bass (**double bass**)	the largest and lowest-pitched member of the string family; measures more than six feet in length, rests on the floor to be played, with the player either standing or sitting on a high stool
cello (**violoncello**)	bass instrument of the string group, much larger than the violin and viola; rests on the floor when played, supported by a spike at the lower end, the player performing seated
K. (Kirkpatric)	one of the numbering systems used to catalog Scarlatti's compositions; named for Ralph Kirkpatric
Longo	another of the numbering systems used to catalog Scarlatti's compositions; named for A. Longo.
viola	slightly larger and lower pitched than the violin; considered the alto member of the string family
violin	the most important and smallest member of the string family; has the most brilliant and singing tone

Suggested Activity: String Family Identification

Purpose: To learn to identify instruments of the string family (violins, violas, cellos, basses) by sight and sound.

Locate a book in your library that presents information about and pictures of instruments from the string family. Find out all you can about them. Look in your area for a music store that might have some of these instruments. Attend concerts where these instruments are played. Find a video that will feature these instruments and music composed especially for them. Look for recordings, audiocassettes, or CDs that feature the string family, and try to identify the instruments by sound. Prepare a game sheet that describes the instruments and have each player identify them.

Quiz

I. Draw lines from the instruments to the proper description:

cello	the largest of the string family instruments
viola	the smallest of the string family instruments
bass	next to largest of the string family instruments
violin	next to smallest of the string family instruments

II. True/false:

_____ 1. Probably the best known of Handel's compositions is *Messiah*.

_____ 2. Handel lived all of his life in southern Russia. *Germany*

_____ 3. Handel was so successful that he had no money worries during his lifetime.

MONTH 4

Franz Joseph Haydn (March 31, 1732–May 31, 1809)

Haydn was born in the tiny Austrian village of Rohrau. His father made wagon wheels and loved to sing folk songs to him. These songs, along with folk dances at festive events, had a powerful influence on his compositions later. His talent in music was recognized, and he was sent to live with a relative who gave him voice lessons. At the age of eight, he went to Vienna to serve as a choirboy in the Cathedral of Saint Stephen until his voice changed. He was then turned out and had a difficult time making a living. For about eight years he gave voice lessons and took odd jobs, including playing the violin in the popular Viennese street bands, while working on his compositions.

At the age of twenty-nine, Haydn began to work for the Esterházy family, the richest and most powerful of the noble Hungarian families. Haydn received a steady income and had the opportunity to have his compositions performed regularly. As a highly skilled servant, Haydn was expected to compose all the music requested by his patron, conduct an orchestra of about twenty-five players, coach singers, and oversee the condition of the instruments and the operation of the music library. For almost thirty years, most of his music was composed for performance in the palaces of the Esterházy family. One isolated palace was equipped with an opera house, a theater, two concert halls, and 126 guest rooms. There were usually two concerts and two opera performances weekly, as well as daily chamber music in the prince's apartment.

Despite his work load, Haydn was an optimistic, good-natured, unselfish, and religious man. He was very conscientious and concerned about his musicians. On one occasion, after the prince had stayed longer than usual at Esterházy, the musicians began to complain to Haydn that they were tired of the remote palace and anxious to get back to Vienna. Haydn composed the

Symphony in F-sharp Minor, now known as the *Farewell Symphony.* During the last movement, one by one, the musicians stopped playing, extinguished their candles, and left the hall until only Haydn and the first violinist were left. The prince got the hint and ordered everyone back to Vienna the next day.

In spite of his relative isolation, Haydn's compositions became popular throughout Europe. After the prince's death in 1790, Haydn was free to travel to London where a concert series had been planned around his compositions. Between 1791 and 1795, Haydn wrote twelve symphonies for performance in London concerts. These symphonies are known as the London Symphonies. He returned to Vienna in 1795, rich and honored. The new prince Esterházy was interested only in religious music, so Haydn agreed to compose a Mass each year. During his late sixties, he composed two well-known oratorios, *The Creation* (1798) and *The Seasons* (1801). Haydn was affectionately called "Papa Haydn" and is also called the father of the symphony (he wrote at least 104 symphonies). He died in 1809 at the age of seventy-seven, while Napoleon's army occupied Vienna. To recognize Haydn's greatness, joining the Viennese at his funeral were French generals and an honor guard of French soldiers.

Suggested Compositions

Symphony No. 45 in F-sharp Minor (The Farewell Symphony). See the previous description.

Symphony No. 94 in G Major (Surprise). This is one of Haydn's London Symphonies. The unexpected surprise feature is the sudden fortissimo crash on a weak beat in the slow second movement. Haydn was fond of startling, novel effects, and he used this one to attract attention away from compositions of his former pupil and current rival, Ignaz Pleyel.

The Creation. During his visit to London, Haydn became acquainted with oratorios, *Messiah* in particular. At the presentation of the "Hallelujah Chorus" he is reported to have wept and declared Handel to be the "master of us all." *The Creation* is based on John Milton's *Paradise Lost* and the Bible. It contains loving depictions of nature and man's joy in the simple life. One of the most famous choruses from *The Creation* is "The Heavens Are Telling."

Related Materials

Young Person's Guide to the Orchestra, by **Benjamin Britten** (1913–76). Britten has taken a theme by Henry Purcell and given each instrument of the orchestra an opportunity to play it alone in a characteristic setting, then together. The piece is delightful and artistic and provides an excellent opportunity to become acquainted with the different timbres of orchestral instruments.

The Orchestra, by Mark Rubin and Alan Daniel, and read by Peter Ustinov. Another delightful way for the whole family to explore the orchestra and orchestral music. Available in video, cassette, CD, or book and audiocassette.

"Glorious Things of Thee Are Spoken," hymn

Vocabulary

bass clarinet   a larger member of the clarinet family having an upturned metal bell and pitched an octave below the regular clarinet

bassoon   the bass member of the oboe family, requiring a tube that is about eight and one-half feet long (the tube is doubled back on itself). The nasal sound is produced by blowing through a double reed.

chamber music   music that is played by a small group in which each instrument plays a part by itself (orchestral music can have several players for each part). Types of chamber music are distinguished by the number of players: trio, quartet, etc.

clarinet   a tube with a straight bore, a bell opening on one end and a beaklike mouthpiece on the other, usually made of wood. Sound is produced by blowing through a reed, a shaped piece of cane attached to the mouthpiece.

contrabass clarinet   a still larger member of the clarinet family and pitched two octaves below the regular clarinet

double bassoon or contrabassoon   the lowest member of the oboe family, requiring a tube almost eighteen feet long (the tube is doubled back on itself four times); pitched one octave lower than the bassoon. The nasal sound is produced by blowing through a double reed.

embouchure   the positioning and shaping of the lips, mouth, and tongue in order to play good tone, true pitch, and proper attack on a wind instrument

English horn   an alto oboe, pitched a fifth below the regular oboe

flute   a tube with a straight bore about two feet long, closed at one end, usually made of silver, pierced with a number of holes that are opened and closed by keys. Sound is produced by blowing across a hole near the closed end.

oboe   a tube with a cone-shaped bore and a bell opening on one end and a double reed at the other. The nasal sound is produced by blowing through the double reed.

orchestration   the manner in which a composer assigns instruments to individual lines and combines sounds in a given work

piccolo   a small flute sounding one octave higher than the regular flute

sonata or sonata-allegro form   a three-part form (A-B-A) used most often in the first movements of sonatas, symphonies, concertos, and chamber music. While related to the other movements of a composition, this movement may be performed alone.

string quartet   a composition of three or more movements (sections) written for two violins, a viola, and a cello

symphony   a composition in three or more movements (sections) written for an orchestra consisting of strings, woodwinds, brass, and/or percussion

theme   a subject, usually melodic, often heard several times in a composition, sometimes disguised

Suggested Activity: Woodwind Family Identification

Purpose: To learn to identify instruments of the woodwind family (piccolos, flutes, clarinets, bass clarinets, contrabass clarinets, oboes, English horns, bassoons, and contrabassoons) by sight and sound.

Locate a book at your library that includes information about and pictures of instruments from the woodwind family. Find out all you can about them. Look in your area for a music store that might have some of these instruments. Attend concerts where these instruments are played. Find a video that will feature these instruments and music composed especially for them. Look for recordings, audiocassettes, or CDs that feature the woodwind family, and try to identify the instruments by sound. Prepare a game sheet that describes the instruments and have each player identify them.

Quiz

Identify the instruments of the woodwind family by drawing lines from the instrument name to the appropriate definition:

flute	double-reed instrument pitched lower than the bassoon
double bassoon	highest-pitched woodwind instrument
English horn	generally made of silver
piccolo	relative of the oboe
clarinet	relative of the English horn

bassoon	highest pitched of the clarinet family
bass clarinet	lowest pitched of the clarinet family
oboe	middle pitched of the clarinet family
contrabass clarinet	requires a tube about eight and one-half feet long

MONTH 5

Wolfgang Amadeus Mozart
(January 27, 1756–December 5, 1791)

Mozart was the most remarkable of musical child prodigies. He was born in Salzburg, Austria. At three, Mozart would seek out pleasing harmonic combinations on the harpsichord, and when he succeeded he shouted with joy. His father began to teach him composition and harpsichord when he was only four. With just a few basic lessons he was soon able to play not only the harpsichord, but also the violin with facility. His musical memory was developed to an extraordinary degree; he could play a composition after hearing it once. His ear was so sensitive that he could identify tones and chords sounded on the piano while he was blindfolded; his musical invention was so rich that he could improvise on a given subject for half an hour. At five he wrote several delightful minuets, still familiar to beginners of piano in our time. At seven he completed a sonata, at eight a symphony.

Mozart's father, Leopold, seized the opportunity to exhibit his wonder child to the world and decided to tour Europe with him. Soon the young genius was being advertised as a "scientific phenomenon." In 1763 Mozart performed a violin concerto. He also accompanied symphonies on a harpsichord or organ whose manual or keyboard was often covered by a cloth. He could name all notes played for him from a distance whether singly or in chords and could improvise in any key on the harpsichord or organ.

His success was indeed phenomenal as he traveled through Europe receiving extravagant commissions for compositions as well as lofty praise and adulation. He returned to Salzburg in 1771 where he lived until 1777. He no longer received the acclaim he had enjoyed and entered into one of the most unhappy periods of his life. He was no longer the child prodigy, and powerful patrons who had once showered him with gifts and praises now ignored him. In 1778, tragedy struck: His mother died.

Mozart left Salzburg for Vienna in 1781 and married Constanze Weber in 1782. The post Mozart expected to receive did not materialize. He was forced to earn his living by giving private music lessons, and the little he earned was hardly enough. His admirers could not obtain for him either permanent employment or lucrative commissions. Mozart wrote pathetic letters to people of high station and to publishers, trying in vain to gain their interest in his works.

Although many of his compositions were successful during his lifetime, many more were ignored. He was oppressed by sickness, poverty, and frustration and died a young man. At the time of his death he was composing his *Requiem* and instructed one of his students on how he wished it to be completed.

Suggested Compositions

"Ah, vous dirais-je" (variations on "Twinkle, Twinkle Little Star"). Mozart uses the familiar tune to create a theme and set of variations for piano. These are not difficult, yet are attractive and pleasant for both performer and listener. It is interesting to listen to Mozart's manipulations of the theme.

Piano Concerto in C Major, K 467. Mozart played a critical role in the development of the piano concerto. His twenty-three concertos were written primarily as display pieces for his own public performances. They contain brilliant flourishes and ceremonious gestures characteristic of eighteenth-century social music. All of them are delightful, but this one in C Major is quite taxing for the pianist, requiring more finger dexterity than usual. It has three movements. Listen for the cadenza at the end of the second movement.

The Marriage of Figaro (Le nozze di Figaro). This is an Italian eighteenth-century comic opera composed in 1786. It has many of the characteristics of other operas of its kind: caricatures of the idiosyncrasies of both aristocrats and commoners, the vanities of ladies, miserly old men, clever servants, deceitful husbands and wives, and bungling doctors, lawyers, and military commanders. In the aria "Dehvieni non tardar," Susannah sings about her love for Figaro. He is listening but doesn't know that she knows he is listening. He thinks she is singing about someone else. The opera was written in Italian, but performances in both Italian and English are available, as are English translations of the Italian.

Eine kleine Nachtmusik (A Little Night Music), K. 525. Mozart's elegance and delicacy of touch are embodied in this serenade for string orchestra. The version we know has four movements—compact, intimate, and beautifully proportioned. Originally there were five movements.

"Jesus, I My Cross Have Taken," hymn

Related Materials

Mozart's Magic Fantasy (Cassette 8203 by Sue Hammond). This tape is based on Mozart's opera *The Magic Flute*. The story involves a child, Sarah, who must confront the forces of good and evil. In the end, Sarah is ready to return to her own world and "step out into the music" of Mozart's great overture. This work received the 1991 Juno Award for Best Children's Recording. (Teacher's Guide Available: 80M07860)

Amadeus. This video will probably be at your video store. It contains many accurate facts and much beautiful music. However, the known events of Mozart's life are embellished somewhat in the film, and the viewer must be aware that it is not entirely factual. There are a couple of scenes that might require the fast-forward technique, but overall, it is quite a good movie.

Sherrill, Elizabeth. "A Father's Prayer." *Guideposts,* June 1991, 28-32. This is a brief article about the life of Mozart.

Vocabulary

cadenza	a section of a composition (usually in a concerto at the end of the first movement) that gives the soloist a chance to show off technical skill in performing difficult runs and arpeggios without the orchestra. Eighteenth-century cadenzas were improvised, often on the spot.
crescendo (cresc.)	a term meaning "gradually louder"
decrescendo (diminuendo) (decresc. or dim.)	terms meaning "gradually softer"
dynamics	gradations of loudness and softness
forte (f)	a term meaning "loud"
fortissimo (ff)	a term meaning "very loud"
mezzo forte (mf)	a term meaning "moderately loud"
mezzo piano (mp)	a term meaning "moderately soft"
mode	a pattern of pitches within an octave that makes up the basic melodic and harmonic content of a composition. Medieval music theory recognized eight modes; by the late 1600s prominence was given to the Ionian (major) and the Aeolian (minor) modes.

piano (p)   a term meaning "soft"

pianissimo   a term meaning "very soft"
   (pp)

√ **scale**   a series of pitches arranged in order from low to high. The distance between pitches can vary to create different kinds of scales.

√ **theme and**   a melody is stated in a straightforward and usually unadorned
   variations   manner and then varied any number of times in succeeding sections. The variations may be in the melody, harmony, rhythm, form, texture, key, mode, meter, tempo, etc.

Suggested Activity: Orchestra Seating Arrangement

Find a picture of a seating arrangement for the modern symphony orchestra.

1. Make table games based on the seating. For example, draw some empty chairs in an orchestral arrangement on a piece of paper with numbers on them; put slips of paper in a box with numbers on them that correspond to the number of seats available. Each player has a turn to draw a number and identify the instrument with the corresponding seat number.

2. Each player has a chance to be the conductor. As *Young Person's Guide to the Orchestra* (see page 120) is played, the conductor points to the imaginary orchestra section as it plays.

Quiz

I. Draw lines from each of the dynamic terms to the proper definition:

fortissimo	soft
crescendo	very soft
piano	medium soft
mezzo piano	medium loud
forte	loud
pianissimo	very loud
mezzo forte	gradually softer
decrescendo	gradually louder

II. True/false:

_____ 1. Mozart had written compositions by the age of five.

_____ 2. Mozart's father discouraged him from seeking a career in music.

_____ 3. Mozart was successful and famous throughout his entire life.

MONTH 6

Ludwig van Beethoven (December 16, 1770–March 26, 1827)

Beethoven was born in 1770 in Bonn, Germany. He is an example of someone who achieved greatness while overcoming many obstacles. His family situation was unhappy, but his talent was recognized. His father was his first
instructor and tried to force his progress and develop another child prodigy
like Mozart. Arrangements were made for him to go to Vienna at the age of
twenty-two to study with the famous Franz Joseph Haydn.

This young genius developed in an era of revolution. His powers as a
pianist took the music-loving aristocracy by storm, and they in turn paid him
well for lessons and gave him gifts of money. He began to lose his hearing in
his late twenties, but in spite of this serious handicap, he continued to write
some of the world's greatest compositions.

Although the piano was invented in 1709 by Cristofori, it was not until
the last part of the century that it really began to replace the harpsichord. During Beethoven's lifetime, the piano was undergoing many of the refinements
that have lasted to our day. Since Beethoven was such a powerful and popular
pianist, many piano manufacturers vied for his endorsement of their products.
Some of the finer refinements of the piano's development are reflected in many
of his thirty-two piano sonatas.

Beethoven labored over his compositions, writing, revising, and rewriting.
Many of the sketches he used in developing his music show the progress he
made through various stages. His personality, perhaps more than most other
composers, is related to and revealed in his music.

Beethoven was important in the development of the symphony and its
forms. Although Haydn is considered to be the "father of the symphony,"
Beethoven took many of his designs and expanded them. His compositions
were generally longer and grander than those of Haydn and Mozart, requiring
larger orchestras and more virtuosic playing. He wrote nine complete symphonies. Other works include eleven overtures, incidental music to plays, five
piano concertos, a violin concerto, nine piano trios and other chamber music,
sixteen string quartets, an oratorio, an opera, two Masses, and a variety of
other compositions, both vocal and instrumental.

Beethoven was a rather eccentric person. Upon meeting him in 1823, Sir
Julius Benedict described him as follows: "If I am not mistaken, on the morning that I saw Beethoven for the first time, Blahetka, the father of the pianist,

directed my attention to a stout, short man with a very red face, small, piercing eyes, and bushy eyebrows, dressed in a very long overcoat which reached nearly to his ankles, who entered the shop [the music store of Steiner and Haslinger] about 12 o'clock. Blahetka asked me: 'Who do you think that is?' and I at once exclaimed: 'It must be Beethoven!' because, notwithstanding the high color of his cheeks and his general untidiness, there was in those small piercing eyes an expression which no painter could render. It was a feeling of sublimity and melancholy combined."

Suggested Compositions

Symphony No. 5 in C Minor. The fifth symphony of Beethoven has been interpreted as the musical projection of his resolution "I will grapple with Fate; it shall not overcome me." The struggle is symbolized by the changing of keys from C minor to C major. The famous opening four notes are heard somewhat disguised in the other three movements as well. Contrary to the usual orchestration that used strings, woodwinds, brass, and kettledrums, Beethoven added the trombone, the piccolo, and the contrabassoon in this symphony.

Sonata, Op. 27, No. 2 in C-sharp Minor (Moonlight). The first movement of this sonata is one of the most widely known of all of Beethoven's thirty-two piano sonatas. The subtitle "Moonlight" does not come from Beethoven but from publishers who borrowed it from an article in which the writer claimed that the title had been prompted by the vision "of a boat on Lake Lucerne by a luminous night." Although Beethoven had never been to Lake Lucerne and did not give it the title, "Moonlight" has remained. It is a delightful piece with lyric expressiveness and rich harmonic color.

String Quartet, Op. 59, No. 1 in F Major. The three quartets of Op. 59 were dedicated to the musical amateur Count Rasumovsky, who was the Russian ambassador to Vienna. He played the second violin in a quartet reputed to be the finest in Europe. As a compliment to the count, Beethoven introduced a Russian melody as the principal theme of the finale of the first quartet. The style of the first quartet was so new that the musicians performing it thought Beethoven was playing a joke on them. Muzio Clementi, a colleague of Beethoven's, reportedly said to him, "Surely you do not consider these works to be music?" With time, musicians and audiences came to realize that Beethoven's innovations were rational and accepted them.

"Für Elise." This well-known piano piece was written in 1810 probably for a girl named Therese Malfatti, the niece of the famous physician Johann Malfatti of Vienna. It is believed that Beethoven was smitten by her and proposed marriage to her in 1810. Elise is believed to be Beethoven's nickname for her. More copies of this piece have been sold than any other of Beethoven's piano works.

"Joyful, Joyful We Adore Thee," hymn and choral finale

Related Materials

Beethoven Lives Upstairs (Cassette 8187 by Sue Hammond). Excerpts of Beethoven's compositions plus a riveting narrative that combine for an interesting story and musical education. Winner of the Notable Children's Recording Awards and 1990 Juno Award for Best Children's Recording. (Teacher's Guide Available: 80M07861)

Canadian Brass (a touring group of musicians). Five brass instruments—two trumpets, horn, trombone/euphonium, and tuba—make up this quintet. These are virtuoso performing musicians who have a lot of fun playing a variety of standard brass literature as well as arrangements and compositions written especially for them. Any of their audiocassettes or CDs will be enjoyable, but a live performance, in a concert hall or even on television, is really wonderful. Their programs are unique and blend fine musicianship with a sense of humor.

Vocabulary

French horn often simply called horn, with funnel-shaped mouthpiece and conical tube, coiled into a spiral shape with a widely flared bell. Sound is made similarly to that of the trumpet. Its use of higher partials of the harmonic series makes precise control of pitch difficult. Pitch is changed with valves and embouchure.

trombone moderately low-range, cup-shaped mouthpiece, cylindrical tube, gradually widening at the bottom to a flared bell. Sound is made similarly to that of the trumpet, and pitch is changed with a slide and embouchure.

trumpet soprano-range brass instrument with cup-shaped mouthpiece, cylindrical tube, gradually widening at the bottom to a slightly flared bell. Sound is made by vibrations of the player's lips, which are pressed together and buzzed against the mouthpiece. Pitch is changed with valves and embouchure.

tuba bass-range, cup-shaped mouthpiece, conical tube, flaring into a large bell. Sound is made similarly to that of the trumpet, and pitch is changed with valves and embouchure.

Suggested Activity: Dynamic Identification

Purpose: To learn to hear subtle differences from very soft sounds (pianissimo) to very loud (fortissimo) sounds.

Prepare a list of about twenty sentences and a box with different dynamic names or symbols inside. The sentences could be definitions of the words at first, then other relevant material, possibly about composers, instruments, etc. Have participants draw a dynamic word (or sign) from the box and read the sentence according to the indicated dynamic level. The other person(s) identify the dynamic level demonstrated. This activity needs at least two people, and works with a larger group divided into teams. (Adapted from Margaret Athey and Gwen Hotchkiss, *A Galaxy of Games* [West Nyack, N.Y.: Parker Publishing, 1975], 174-5.)

Quiz

I. Draw lines from each instrument to the proper definition:

tuba	the highest of the brass instruments
trombone	the lowest of the brass instruments
trumpet	the next to lowest of the brass instruments
French horn	the next to highest of the brass instruments

II. True/false:

_____ T ____ 1. Beethoven was quite eccentric.

_____ F ____ 2. Beethoven went blind at an early age.

_____ 3. Beethoven completed nine symphonies.

MONTH 7

Felix Mendelssohn-Bartholdy
(February 3, 1809–November 4, 1847)

Mendelssohn, as he is commonly called, was born in Hamburg, Germany, into a cultured, wealthy family. His grandfather was a famous philosopher and his father a successful banker. He was encouraged to pursue his precocious musical talent. His life was not clouded by financial hardship or personal torment as were many of the leading composers of the Romantic era. He had a happy and successful marriage.

When he was only seventeen, he composed his overture to Shakespeare's *A Midsummer Night's Dream* and, years later, added twelve short pieces that comprised the "incidental music" for a performance of the play at Potsdam in 1843. It is from this incidental music that the "Wedding March" often heard today as a recessional at weddings is taken. At the age of twenty-six, he was conductor of the Gewandhaus Orchestra at Leipzig. He founded the Conservatory of Leipzig. During World War II, the Third Reich tried to ban the performance of his music because he was Jewish, and a statue of Mendelssohn in front of the Conservatory was destroyed.

Mendelssohn enjoyed success as a composer and conductor. He was especially loved in England, where his oratorio *Elijah* was performed. He became close friends with the young Queen Victoria and Prince Albert.

Mendelssohn died at the age of thirty-eight. During his short lifetime, he wrote five symphonies, a violin concerto, several concert overtures, chamber music, songs, oratorios, and keyboard music. He was gifted in many areas— as a composer, conductor, pianist, and educator—and perhaps the taxing of his energies caused his early death.

Suggested Compositions

Concerto for Violin and Orchestra in E Minor. This concerto was composed in 1844 and stands as a staple in violin repertoire today. The work reveals his special gifts: clarity of form and grace of utterance, a subtle orchestral palette and a vein of sentiment that is tender but reserved. This is an exciting concerto, requiring virtuosic technique of the violinist.

A Midsummer Night's Dream (Overture and Incidental Music). Of the twelve pieces added in the incidental music, the "Scherzo," "Nocturne," and "Wedding March" have achieved worldwide popularity and are frequently performed together with the overture as a suite.

"Hark, the Herald Angels Sing," hymn

Related Materials

Erlkönig (The Erlking), by **Franz Schubert** (1797–1828). He wrote for a variety of instruments but is best known for his more than six hundred *Lieder* (German art songs). The *Erlkönig* was written when he was eighteen years old and is based on a famous ballad by the poet Goethe. The text is based on a legend that says whoever is touched by the King of the Elves must die. The poem has four characters: the narrator, the father, the child, and the elf. The piano accompaniment enhances the drama of the text.

Impromptu in A-flat, Op. 90, No. 4, by Schubert. This piece was written in 1827 and is in three sections, with each section subdividing into smaller sections. Impromptu means "on the spur of the moment" and usually is given to pieces that occur to the composer in a flash of inspiration. This is one of Schubert's most popular piano pieces.

Vocabulary

bass drum largest of the orchestral drums; consists of a wooden shell almost three feet in diameter, covered with skin, and played vertically; struck with a bass-drum beater whose ends are padded with wool or felt

castanets a pair of shell-shaped wooden clappers, usually attached to a long handle

celeste keyboard instrument resembling a small portable piano; has a four-octave range; played with traditional piano technique; hammers strike metal bars; can play multiple keys simultaneously

chimes a graduated series of metal tubes suspended from a frame and struck with a wooden or hard leather–covered hammer; tone is much deeper than that of the bells; often used in imitation of the church bells

cymbal metal plate from fourteen to twenty inches in diameter usually made of brass with a leather handle; played in pairs or suspended and struck

definite pitch sound heard at a particular frequency and identified with a letter name (A, B, C, etc.)

gong a large bronze disk about three to four feet in diameter, suspended, and struck in the center by a mallet

indefinite pitch sound in which no particular frequency predominates, such as that of a snare drum, tambourine, etc.

marimba a mallet instrument that originated in Africa and was developed in Latin America; consists of tuned wooden bars suspended over resonators

orchestra bells (German glockenspiel) a set of bars made of bell metal of graduated sizes placed on a frame in two series that are similar to the white and black keys of the piano; struck by hard rubber or wooden mallets, producing high, bell-like tones

overture an instrumental introduction to a longer work, such as an opera, oratorio, or play

✓ **piano**	keyboard instrument consisting of eighty-eight keys and strings that are struck by hammers; invented in 1709 and developed through the eighteenth and early nineteenth centuries; originally called the pianoforte because it was the first keyboard that could play a range of dynamics. Upright pianos have vertical sound-boards and strings, grand pianos have horizontal soundboards and strings.
snare drum	a small cylindrical drum with a shell made of metal and a head of plastic or leather, ranging in size from twelve to eighteen inches in diameter and from three to twenty inches in depth
tambourine	a shallow drum consisting of wooden hoop and parchment head; small metal discs attached to the hoop rattle when the instrument is struck, rubbed, or shaken
timpani	tuned drums, consisting of a shell usually made of copper or brass, with a head of calfskin stretched across the opening. The head can be tightened or loosened by screws turned by hand or by pedals, changing the pitch.
tom-tom	a high pitched drum that originated with various Native Americans
triangle	a steel rod bent into the shape of a triangle and played with a metal beater, either inside or outside the triangle
xylophone	consists of a graduated series of wooden bars suspended on a frame in two rows similar to the white and black keys of the piano; usually played with hard mallets; gives the sound of the rattling of skeleton bones

Suggested Activity: Percussion Family Identification

Purpose: To learn to identify instruments of the percussion family (see vocabulary list) by sight and sound.

Locate a book at your library that includes information about and pictures of instruments from the percussion family. Find out all you can about them. Look in your area for a music store that might have some of these instruments. Attend concerts where these instruments are played. Find a video that will feature these instruments and music composed especially for them. Look for recordings, audiocassettes, or CDs that feature the percussion family and try to identify the various instruments. Prepare a game sheet that describes the instruments and have each player identify the instruments.

Quiz

I. Unscramble the following percussion instrument words. The upper case letters are the beginning of each word.

moT-moT	laCmyb	nogG
naPio	gianTrel	ramMiba
miChes	lelsB	miTnapi
saBmsurD	raneSmurD	staCetans

II. True/false:

_____ 1. Mendelssohn was born into poverty.

_____ 2. Mendelssohn lived to the age of seventy-five.

_____ 3. One of Mendelssohn's most famous compositions is his Violin Concerto.

MONTH 8

Frédéric Chopin (February 22, 1810–October 17, 1849)

Chopin was born near Warsaw, Poland. His father was French, his mother Polish. He was educated at his father's school for sons of the Polish nobility, where he acquired a taste for the aristocratic lifestyle. After winning acclaim in Poland as a pianist, he traveled in Europe giving concerts and eventually settled in Paris in 1831. There he established himself as a preeminent pianist and composer. He moved among the aristocracy and taught their children.

Chopin was a composer of character pieces for the piano. He was a miniaturist, writing short pieces and infusing them with traits of the Romantic era. He was often called the "poet of the piano." He uncovered many qualities of the piano by exploiting its range and extending its harmonies with bass tones sustained by the pedal. "Everything must be made to sing," he told his pupils. He included delicate ornaments in his music, enhancing the melodic line. He wrote several of each of the following: nocturnes, waltzes, mazurkas, preludes, ballads, scherzos, polonaises, impromptus, etudes, as well as three sonatas and two concertos. All of his music demands not only a flawless touch and technique, but also imaginative use of the pedals and a careful use of tempo rubato, which Chopin himself described as a slight pushing ahead or holding back.

Chopin was able to exploit the piano in ways untried by earlier composers. He created widely spaced chords in the bass to be sustained by the pedal, making new masses of tone to support his lyrical, ornamented melodies. These melodies are basically vocal rather than instrumental and possibly were influenced by the great *Lieder* composer, Schubert. His ideas about harmony were unusual for the early part of the century, and they influenced many later composers.

Chopin remained under the influence of the French writer George Sand (Mme. Aurore Dudevant) for about seven years. He also knew Franz Liszt and the poet Heinrich Heine. Toward the end of his life he became ill with consumption. Weakened by a concert tour in England and Scotland, he died in Paris at the age of thirty-nine.

Suggested Compositions

Revolutionary Etude, Op. 10, No. 12. Chopin was touring Germany when he received the news that Warsaw had fallen to the Russians. His first impulse was to return to Poland and fight, but he was discouraged from doing so and decided to spread his patriotic feelings through music.

Fantasy-Impromptu, Op. 66. One of the better-known piano pieces of Chopin. Contains the theme from which "I'm Always Chasing Rainbows" was derived. A very passionate work.

Etude in A Minor, Op. 25, No. 11. Chopin was among the first of the composers to combine the usual qualities of an etude—a study primarily for the development of technique—with significant artistic content. This etude, titled the "Winter Wind" long after Chopin's death, opens with a simple eight-note melody, played very slowly (lento), then bursts with rapid passages in both hands, demanding accuracy, speed, and endurance from the pianist. The work is short, but one is easily swept by the tremendous drive and the explosive force of the music.

Related Materials

Franz Liszt (1811–86). Liszt wrote many virtuosic pieces for the piano including *Transcendental Etudes,* based on Niccolò Paganini violin pieces. There are twelve etudes, some given descriptive titles. They are very difficult to perform.

Hungarian Rhapsodies, by Liszt. These compositions, originally for piano, are among Liszt's most performed works. Instrumental arrangements for a wide variety of instruments, including harmonica, jazz band, and full orchestra, have been made of these works. Number 2 is a particular favorite.

Vocabulary

ballade	an extended piece for the piano, usually in three-part form, possibly inspired by literary models
barcarole	a boat song in moderate 6/8 or 12/8 meter with a repeated accompaniment figure
berceuse	a lullaby or cradle song, usually in 6/8 meter with a patterned accompaniment
character pieces	short nineteenth-century piano pieces, published under a variety of titles, some of them descriptive
etude	a study piece designed to develop technical proficiency
impromptu	a French term for a nineteenth-century piano piece that sounds as though it could have been improvised
mazurka	a Polish dance in moderate triple meter with the accent usually on the second or third beat
nocturne	a slow piece with a strong melody, usually in the right hand, and a quiet accompaniment
polonaise	a Polish dance of noble character in moderate triple meter with distinctive rhythmic patterns
prelude	a keyboard piece in a free style used as a preface to a fugue or suite in the Baroque period; in the Romantic era, the prelude became an entity in itself.
rubato	a direction to perform in a slightly free tempo or rhythm by altering the duration of the notes; literally means "in robbed time"
scherzo	sometimes the third movement in a four-movement sonata and, in the case of Beethoven, whimsical and humorous in character; as used by Chopin, a long, freestanding piece that is more tragic in nature
waltz	a dance in moderate triple meter that originated around 1800

Suggested Activity: Name That Tune

Purpose: To learn themes and their sources from important compositions.

Play either on the piano, or other instrument, or with a recording, audio-cassette, or CD, the opening section of one of the pieces listed in this category (then other categories, then a mix of categories), and give points to the person who can identify the title of the composition, with extra points for the identification of the composer.

Quiz

I. Unscramble the following words that are used to describe some of Chopin's music. The uppercase letters are the beginning or each word.

duteE   zerchoS   kurzaMa   daleBal

zWatl   dulereP   esolinoPa   Nunteroc

II. True/false:

_____1. Chopin was born and educated in Poland but moved later to Paris.

_____2. Chopin is famous for piano compositions.

_____3. Chopin lived to the age of sixty-five.

MONTH 9

Robert Schumann (June 8, 1810–July 29, 1856)

Schumann was born in Zwickau, Germany. His father was a publisher, bookseller, and writer who wanted his son to study law. However, young Schumann's love was music and literature. As a boy, he was an accomplished pianist and writer of articles and poems. He entered Leipzig University to study law but attended few classes. He spent his time in musical, social, and literary activity.

In 1829 he engaged the eminent teacher Friedrich Wieck for piano study in Leipzig. He moved to Wieck's home, where he studied piano and music theory. His teacher felt that he had a promising career as a concert pianist ahead of him, but when Schumann injured the fourth finger of his right hand on a contrivance he had made to exercise his fingers, his performing career ended.

He pursued his interest in writing and in his twenties wrote most of his piano music. He, along with some of his like-minded friends, founded a journal named *The New Magazine for Music*. Schumann enthusiastically poured his energies into editing the periodical that, under his direction, became one of the most important music journals in Europe.

Wieck's daughter, Clara, was nine when Schumann moved to their home. It was when she reached the age of sixteen that Schumann realized he loved her. Clara was a concert pianist who was very devoted to her father; yet she loved Robert. Although Wieck opposed their marriage, it took place in 1840 when Clara was twenty-one and Robert thirty. That year he produced more than a hundred songs.

Clara became the main performer of Schumann's piano works, and their fame spread throughout Europe. In spite of his success and the love of his wife and children, he began to withdraw from the world and by 1844 had experienced a severe breakdown. He recovered temporarily but by 1854 could no longer function professionally. He died two years later.

Although he composed for orchestra, Schumann is best known for his piano music and his *Lieder*. He most often grouped several short piano pieces (character pieces) together to form collections with rather romantic titles such as *Fantasy Pieces, Papillons (Butterflies), Romances,* and *Scenes from Childhood.* The favorite topic for his *Lieder* was love, and he used many texts written by his favorite poet, Heinrich Heine. In addition to the piano music and *Lieder,* he composed four symphonies.

Suggested Compositions

Piano Concerto in A Minor. Clara first performed this concerto in 1846. It is a favorite of today's audiences, and it has been recorded by many artists.

Symphony No. 1 in B-flat. This symphony is called the *Spring Symphony* because it was Schumann's intention at one time to give a descriptive title to each of the movements. The first movement is called "Spring's Awakening" and the last is called "Spring's Farewell." The names are appropriate, and the music is fresh, energetic, and spontaneous.

Carnaval, Op. 9, is a musical composition for the piano that represents a festive collection of people in various disguises—Chopin, the violinist Paganini, Schumann's girlfriends, and Schumann himself. In some of his pieces he also represents the two sides of his personality, whom he called "Florestan" (the impetuous one) and "Eusebius" (the reflective one).

"Ich grolle nicht" is probably Schumann's most powerful love song and is based on a text by Heine. It is a good example of the Romantic spirit: soaring melody and sustained dissonances in the accompaniment. Although it is most often sung in German, translations are almost always available in the notes accompanying recordings, audiocassettes, or CDs. (Songs are usually performed in the original language because of translation difficulties. If the translation is literal, it is awkward at best in English; if it is translated correctly, the meshing of the words with the music is awkward.)

Related Materials

Richard Wagner (1813–83). Wagner is best known for his orchestral compositions and operas. One of the best-known operas, *Tristan und Isolde,* contains a well-known "Prelude" and the beautiful "Love Duet" in the final scene.

Giuseppe Verdi (1813–1901). Verdi is best known for his operas that included *Il travatore, Rigoletto, La traviata, Aida, Otello,* and *Falstaff. Aida* is often called "the perfect grand opera." The plot and the music require dramatic staging effects.

Vocabulary

beat	the unit used to measure musical time
dotted note	a note head with a small dot to the right, indicating that one-half of the note's value should be added to its duration
eighth note	a blackened head with a stem and a flag; usually one-half beat
half note	an open head with a stem; usually two beats
head	the circular part of the note that, when placed on a line or space, indicates the pitch
note	a symbol used to write music on a staff, indicating time value for each pitch and consisting of a stem (a whole note does not have a stem) and a head
quarter note	a blackened head with a stem; usually one beat
stem	the vertical line attached to the note head on half, quarter, eighth, etc., notes, indicating the duration
whole note	an open head, indicating the longest note value most often used in modern notation; usually four beats

Suggested Activity: Note Value Identification

Purpose: To distinguish the various note values by sign and duration.

Create musical equations with note values. Can be played as teams or individually. Difficulty can be adjusted according to the age and progress of the players. Here are some examples; you can create more of your own.

whole note – _____   = half note

_____ + _____   = whole note

_____ + _____ + _____   = dotted half note

Quiz

I. Draw a line from the following words to the proper definition:

dotted note	usually gets one beat
eighth note	usually gets four beats
quarter note	usually gets a half beat
half note	usually gets two beats
whole note	adds one half of a note's value to its total value

II. True/false:

_____ 1. Schumann married his teacher's daughter.

_____ 2. Schumann was also a journalist and editor.

_____ 3. Schumann hurt his hand in an exercise device.

MONTH 10

Johannes Brahms
(May 7, 1833–April 3, 1897)

Brahms was born in Hamburg, Germany, the son of a double bass player. He learned to play the piano early, made rapid progress, and was sent to study with a famous pianist and composer in Hamburg. At an early age, he met the virtuoso violist, Joseph Joachim, who was impressed with his early compositions and introduced him to Robert Schumann. Schumann recognized the shy composer as a future leader and published an article in his journal, naming Brahms as a new, young, leading composer of absolute music, a tradition of purely musical expression that does not contain the elements of nonmusical implications, such as programmatic titles and literary and visual arts references.

Clara and Robert Schumann took the younger Brahms into their home in 1854, where he lived for some time. He helped Clara through the ordeal of Robert's illness and death. Brahms moved to Vienna in 1863. Clara and Johannes remained lifelong friends.

Brahms fought what he considered to be softness in himself and became feared for his caustic wit. To a musician fishing for compliments he remarked, "Yes, you have talent. But very little!" To elderly ladies whom he was rehearsing in *The Creation* (composed by Haydn in 1798) he admonished: "Why do you drag it so? Surely you took this much faster under Haydn."

Brahms looked on himself as a preserver of tradition. He differs significantly from his innovative contemporaries, Berlioz, Liszt, and Wagner. He was regarded in his day as a musical conservative. He used forms from the Baroque and Classical eras yet combined them with full, sumptuous textures and intricate weavings and transformings of motifs and themes. Brahms worked and reworked his compositions and let nothing survive that he thought was inferior. He constantly revised his works. During his lifetime he composed four symphonies and a variety of chamber, piano, and choral music as well as many *Lieder*.

Suggested Compositions

"Hungarian Dance No. 5" is the fifth in a series of twenty-one pieces written for four hands, one piano. This is an arrangement of a Hungarian Gypsy song, and is rhythmic, driving, flamboyant, and just plain fun.

Wiegenlied. This is the famous and well-loved "Brahms's Lullaby" in its original setting, written for voice and piano.

Symphony No. 1 in C Minor, Op. 68. Brahms started on this composition in 1855, when he was only twenty-two years of age, but it was not until 1876 that the whole work was ready for performance. By that time the world had come to see Brahms as the successor to Beethoven in the field of instrumental music. It was first performed in Karlsruhe and later that same year was played in Vienna. The symphony has four movements.

"Savior Hear Us When We Pray," hymn

Related Materials

Composers of the following also used elements of nationalism in their compositions:

New World Symphony was written by the Czechoslovakian composer **Antonin Dvořák** (1841–1904) after he had visited America and became acquainted with the music of American blacks. Some feel that he includes references to songs such as "Swing Low, Sweet Chariot" (movement one) and "Going Home" (movement two) in this work.

Peer Gynt Suite was written by **Edvard Grieg** (1843–1907) of Norway and contains eight of the twenty-three originally composed pieces for Ibsen's *Peer Gynt.* (Also well known is his *Piano Concerto in A Minor.*)

The Moldau or *Vltava* was written by the Czechoslovakian composer **Bedřich Smetana** (1824–84) and is a tone poem about the famous river that flows through Prague. This composition contains a program written by the composer and mixes musical imagery with patriotic associations.

Vocabulary

adagio	very slow but faster than largo
allegro	a fast, happy tempo
andante	slow
half step (tone)	the smallest interval commonly used in Western music; on the piano the distance between two adjacent keys, black or white
largo	very, very slow; literally means "broad"

Lieder	German art songs for solo voice with piano accompaniment, written by Schubert, Schumann, Wolf, Brahms, and other German composers
moderato	a moderate, walking tempo
presto	a very, very fast tempo
rhapsody	a title used for a short piano piece free in form and expressing a particular theme (for example, patriotism, based on folk songs, etc.)
tempo	rate of speed
vivace	very fast

Suggested Activity: Tempo Identification

Purpose: To understand the meaning of the words commonly used for tempo designation.

Have the names of the various tempos listed individually on cards. Without looking at the card, one player draws a card and gives it to another player. He must try to guess the name on the card by asking questions.

Quiz

True/false:

_____ 1. Brahms lived and died in Germany.

_____ 2. Brahms wrote music only for the piano.

_____ 3. Brahms's musical style was very untraditional.

_____ 4. Brahms and the Schumanns were good friends.

_____ 5. Brahms wrote his music very quickly and did not see any need to rework his compositions.

MONTH 11

Camille Saint-Saëns
(October 9, 1835–December 16, 1921)

Saint-Saëns was one of the most important musicians in France during the turn of the century. As a small child, he heard music in the sounds around him. He started piano lessons at the age of two and showed brilliant talent. He performed publicly at age five and composed his first piece at age six. His compositions included several operas, songs, keyboard pieces, five symphonies, three violin concertos, two cello concertos, and five piano concertos. He retained the French characteristics of lyricism and lightheartedness while introducing some German technical ideas and larger forms to his music. He was a composer, concert pianist, organist, conductor, poet, teacher, and author. He became so famous during his lifetime that he had to wear disguises to escape attention.

Suggested Compositions

Carnival of the Animals. This work consists of fourteen pieces for two pianos and orchestra, each piece representing a different animal, including chickens, birds, fish, elephants, and a kangaroo. The piece about the swan (French: *Le cygne*) is one of the most famous, and the one called "The Pianist" depicts a poor creature locked in a cage and playing scales all day. Ogden Nash added comical verse for each section that gave even more humor to the piece. Some recordings include Nash's words. You can probably find recordings with or without Nash's verses at your library.

Samson and Delilah. This work is an opera based on the biblical account of Samson and Delilah. The story is somewhat romanticized and is a bit heavy in its totality for children but contains some beautiful melodies that they can enjoy.

Danse Macabre. This work is a composition for orchestra with a program of events that take place in a graveyard. The colorful orchestration suggests the spooky wild dance of departed spirits and their return to their graves at dawn. This is a good example of music that attempts to describe the object or scene suggested by the title of the composition.

Related Materials

Georges Bizet (1838–75). Bizet is best remembered for his opera *Carmen.* Two of the best-known pieces from this opera are the "Toreador Song" and "Habanera," which are based on tango rhythms.

Giacomo Puccini (1858–1924). Puccini is best known for his operas, especially *La Bohème* and *Madame Butterfly.* Each of his operas represents years of work and endless revisions.

Vocabulary

absolute music	music that exists for its own sake; does not tell a story; also called "abstract music" or "pure music"
major	one of the two basic modes of Western music from about 1600; consists of W W H W W W H steps (whole step = W; half step = H)

minor	another of the two basic modes upon which most of the scales of Western music from about 1600 are based; consists of W H W W H W W steps (whole step = W; half step = H)
octave	the eighth-scale degree above or below any tone
program music	a term referring to music that tells a story. Sometimes the story is very specific and written as part of the composition, and at other times it is general, with the music merely suggesting a story. Also called "descriptive music."
symphonic poem	an important nineteenth-century form for orchestra, generally in one rather long movement, with a title that suggests a subject, story, or "program"
tone poem	another name for symphonic poem
whole step (tone)	the second smallest interval commonly used in Western music equal to two half steps. On the piano it is the distance between two keys with one key between, black or white.

Suggested Activity: Music Symbol Identification

Purpose: To reinforce the use and meaning of music symbols.

Each player has a piece of paper and draws a large tick-tack-toe on it. The leader then calls out nine music symbols. Each player draws each symbol as it is called in the area of his choice. After all the symbols are drawn, the play begins. The same symbols are called one by one again by the leader in a different order and crossed out by each player. The first player to cross out any three symbols in a straight line (horizontal, vertical, or diagonal) is the winner.

Quiz

Draw a line from each word to the definition that is most appropriate:

whole step	moves from one key to the very next
program music	skips one key
half step	music that suggests a story
tone poem	an orchestral piece that suggests a story

MONTH 12

Peter Ilyich Tchaikovsky (May 7, 1840–November 6, 1893)

Tchaikovsky was born in the Russian province of Vyatka. His father was a mining engineer and factory manager. In 1848 the family moved to Saint

Petersburg (later known as Leningrad) where Peter attended law school. After graduation and his mother's death in 1854, he began to compose seriously. In 1863 he returned to school, this time at the Saint Petersburg Conservatory, and studied composition with Anton Rubenstein. Rubenstein was cosmopolitan and concerned himself with standard directions of European music. There was, however, a movement in Russia toward nationalistic folk traditions. A group of five Russian composers in Saint Petersburg—Balakirev, Borodin, Cui, Mussorgsky, and Rimsky-Korsakov—invited Tchaikovsky to join their group (the Russian Five) and help promote their ideas. However, since he was now teaching at the new conservatory in Moscow, and since he did not share their views enthusiastically, Tchaikovsky declined. The trend toward nationalism did influence Tchaikovsky, however, and it can be particularly noticed in his operas and his fantasy overture, "Romeo and Juliet" (1869).

Part of Tchaikovsky's life was unhappy. He experienced a failed marriage, among other things, and it was during these times of turmoil that he wrote his most significant works. He was encouraged by his patroness, Nadezhda von Meck, who gave him financial and moral support by correspondence on the condition that they never meet. Her support allowed Tchaikovsky to devote himself full time to composition.

Tchaikovsky wrote seven operas, three ballets, six symphonies, three concertos (piano, violin), two overtures, suites, and variations, chamber, choral, and piano music as well as songs. The ballets, the last three symphonies, and the piano concerto are especially well known today.

Suggested Compositions

The *1812 Overture* was written in 1880. It is a delightful piece that demonstrates Tchaikovsky's innovative orchestral techniques.

The Nutcracker Suite is a collection of short pieces from the *Nutcracker* ballet that includes a miniature overture, a march, the "Dance of the Sugarplum Fairy," "Trepek," "Arab Dance," "Chinese Dance," "Dance of the Toy Flutes," and "Waltz of the Flowers." The music stands alone very well, and good recordings are available. This magical suite is very often performed just prior to Christmas, and attending a live performance is an excellent family activity. The music and ballet can also be found on video and the music on a variety of records, tapes, and compact discs.

Piano Concerto No. 1 in B-flat Minor. A well-loved composition for piano and orchestra. It has three movements and again demonstrates Tchaikovsky's mastery of orchestration.

Related Materials

Pictures at an Exhibition, by **Modest Mussorgsky** (1839–81). This set of ten "sound pictures" was composed after Mussorgsky visited a memorial exhibition of an artist friend, Victor Hartmann. These pictures are tied together with a recurring melody called the "Promenade," which represents the viewer moving from picture to picture. Even though the visual pictures have been forgotten, the music lives on. The movements or pictures are titled as follows: Picture I: "Gnome," Picture II: "The Ruined Castle," Picture III: "The Tuileries Gardens," Picture IV: "The Polish Ox-Cart," Picture V: "Ballet of Unhatched Chicks," Picture VI: "Samuel Goldenberg and Schmule," Picture VII: "The Market at Limoges," Picture VIII: "The Roman Catacombes," Picture IX: "The Hut of the Witch, Baba Yaga," Picture X: "The Great Gate at Kiev."

Scheherazade, by **Nicolai Rimsky-Korsakov** (1844–1908). This is a symphonic suite composed in 1888. It is a fine example of Rimsky-Korsakov's genius for orchestration.

"Polovetsian Dances," by **Aleksandr Borodin** (1831–87). These dances are from Act 2 of his opera *Prince Igor* and illustrate the harmonies, bright colors, and exotic oriental flavor that characterize much of Russian music from this period. These dances are often performed in a concert version apart from the opera.

Vocabulary

bell lyre like a glockenspiel but portable; the player holds the frame by the handle and uses a single beater on the bars

cornet similar to a trumpet in range and general sound; tone is less penetrating than that of the trumpet; mainly used in bands

euphonium shaped like a tuba but smaller with a baritone range; has three or four valves, conical bore

flügelhorn like the cornet but with a wider conical bore with three valves; comes in several sizes and is occasionally part of the orchestra

mellophone a brass instrument used to substitute for the French horn; has three valves, looks much like the French horn, but is easier to play

saxophone a single-reed instrument, invented about 1840, and with characteristics of both the clarinet and oboe; uses the same type of mouthpiece as the clarinet, and a single reed but has a conical bore and flared bell like the oboe; four types of saxophones are grouped by range: soprano, alto, tenor, and baritone; used in bands and occasionally as part of the orchestra

sousaphone   a large bass tuba, held so that it encircles the player's body. Invented by John Philip Sousa especially for marching bands; usually made from lightweight material.

symphonic band   An ensemble that uses wind, brass, and percussion instruments, and sometimes cellos and double basses. Intended to be more versatile than marching bands, parade bands, etc., symphonic bands perform concert literature.

Suggested Activity: Band Instrument Identification

Purpose: To learn to identify band instruments (see vocabulary list) by sight and sound.

Locate a book at your library that includes information about and pictures of band instruments. Find out all you can about them. Look in your area for a music store that might have some of these instruments. Attend concerts where these instruments are played and music is composed especially for them. Look for recordings, tapes, or compact discs that feature band instruments and try to identify them. Prepare a game sheet that describes the instruments and have each player identify them.

Quiz

Fill in the blanks:

Tchaikovsky was born in the country of _____. Two of his most famous compositions are the ballet called _____ and the concerto for _____ and orchestra in B-flat minor. The Nationalistic movement influenced Tchaikovsky, although he did not join the Russian _____. He was also influenced by his teacher, the famous Anton _____.

Time Line of Selected Composers

Although there is a body of significant music written prior to the Baroque era, this listing begins with Corelli. Included are selected composers of the Baroque, Classical, Romantic, Impressionist, and twentieth-century eras.

Music in this survey is largely drawn from a common practice that began in the 1600s and continued into the 1900s. This time span is so named because its composers accepted a common theoretical basis of chord progressions for their writing. Some of the twentieth-century composers listed use styles no longer bound by traditional theory. Compositions written earlier than 1600 are less accessible to young listeners and so have not been included.

Also included is a list of composers by their birth dates so you can choose a composer's birthday to celebrate.

CHRONOLOGICAL ORDER

Baroque (circa 1600–1750)

Arcangelo Corelli	(1653–1713)
Henry Purcell	(1659–1695)
Antonio Vivaldi	(1678–1741)
Johann Sebastian Bach	(1685–1750)
George Frideric Handel	(1685–1759)
Domenico Scarlatti	(1685–1757)
Carl Philipp Emanuel Bach	(1714–1788)

Classical (circa 1750–1800)

Carl Philipp Emanuel Bach	(1714–1788)
Franz Joseph Haydn	(1732–1809)
Wolfgang Amadeus Mozart	(1756–1791)
Ludwig van Beethoven	(1770–1827)

Romantic (circa 1800–1900)

Ludwig van Beethoven	(1770–1827)
Gioacchino Rossini	(1792–1868)
Franz Schubert	(1797–1828)
Hector Berlioz	(1803–1869)
Felix Mendelssohn	(1809–1847)
Frédéric Chopin	(1810–1849)
Robert Schumann	(1810–1856)
Franz Liszt	(1811–1886)
Richard Wagner	(1813–1883)
Giuseppe Verdi	(1813–1901)
Bedřich Smetana	(1824–1884)
Johannes Brahms	(1833–1897)
Aleksandr Borodin	(1833–1887)
Camille Saint-Saëns	(1835–1921)
Georges Bizet	(1838–1875)
Modest Mussorgsky	(1839–1881)
Peter (Pyotr) Ilyich Tchaikovsky	(1840–1893)
Antonin Dvořák	(1841–1904)
Edvard Grieg	(1843–1907)
Nicolai Rimsky-Korsakov	(1844–1908)
Giacomo Puccini	(1858–1924)
Gustav Mahler	(1860–1911)
Richard Strauss	(1864–1949)
Jean Sibelius	(1865–1957)

Impressionist (circa 1880–1940)

Claude Debussy	(1862–1918)
Maurice Ravel	(1875–1937)
Charles Griffes	(1884–1920)

Twentieth Century (1900–Present)

Arnold Schoenberg	(1874–1951)
Charles Ives	(1874–1954)
Béla Bartók	(1881–1945)
Igor Stravinsky	(1882–1971)
Sergei Prokofiev	(1891–1953)
Ferde Grofé	(1892–1972)
Henry Cowell	(1897–1965)
George Gershwin	(1898–1937)
Aaron Copland	(1900–1990)
Dimitri Shostakovich	(1906–1975)
Samuel Barber	(1910–1981)
John Cage	(1912–1992)
Benjamin Britten	(1913–1976)
Leonard Bernstein	(1918–1990)
Mario Davidovsky	(1934–)
Steve Reich	(1936–)

Jazz/Broadway

Scott Joplin	(1868–1917)
William Christopher Handy	(1873–1958)
Irving Berlin	(1888–1989)
Paul Whiteman	(1890–1967)
Lorenz (Larry) Hart	(1895–1943)
Oscar Hammerstein	(1895–1960)
Ira Gershwin	(1896–1983)
Duke Ellington	(1899–1974)
Louis Armstrong	(1901–1971)
Guy Lombardo	(1902–1977)
Richard Rodgers	(1902–1979)
Jimmy Dorsey	(1904–1957)
Glenn Miller	(1904–1944)
Frederick Loewe	(1901–1988)
Tommy Dorsey	(1905–1956)
Benny Goodman	(1909–1986)
Harry James	(1916–1983)
Alan J. Lerner	(1918–1986)

COMPOSERS' BIRTHDAYS

January

Wolfgang Amadeus Mozart	(January 27, 1756)
Franz Schubert	(January 31, 1797)

February

Felix Mendelssohn	(February 3, 1809)
Arcangelo Corelli	(February 17, 1653)
George Frideric Handel	(February 23, 1685)
Jimmy Dorsey	(February 29, 1904)
Gioacchino Rossini	(February 29, 1792)

March

Frédéric Chopin	(March 1, 1810)
Glenn Miller	(March 1, 1904)
Bedřich Smetana	(March 2, 1824)
Mario Davidovsky	(March 4, 1934)
Antonio Vivaldi	(March 4, 1678)
Maurice Ravel	(March 7, 1875)
C. P. E. Bach	(March 8, 1714)
Samuel Barber	(March 9, 1910)
Henry Cowell	(March 11, 1897)
Nicolai Rimsky-Korsakov	(March 18, 1844)
Johann Sebastian Bach	(March 21, 1685)
Modest Mussorgsky	(March 21, 1839)
Béla Bartók	(March 25, 1881)
Ferde Grofé	(March 27, 1892)
Paul Whiteman	(March 28, 1890)
Franz Joseph Haydn	(March 31, 1732)

April

Sergei Prokofiev	(April 23, 1891)
Duke Ellington	(April 29, 1899)

May

Lorenz (Larry) Hart	(May 2, 1895)
Johannes Brahms	(May 7, 1833)
Peter Ilyich Tchaikovsky	(May 7, 1840)
Irving Berlin	(May 11, 1888)
Richard Wagner	(May 22, 1813)
Benny Goodman	(May 30, 1909)

June

Robert Schumann	(June 8, 1810)
Frederick Loewe	(June 10, 1904)
Richard Strauss	(June 11, 1864)
Edvard Grieg	(June 15, 1843)
Igor Stravinsky	(June 17, 1882)
Richard Rodgers	(June 28, 1902)

July

Gustav Mahler	(July 7, 1860)
Oscar Hammerstein	(July 12, 1895)

August

Leonard Bernstein	(August 15, 1918)
Claude Debussy	(August 22, 1862)
Alan J. Lerner	(August 31, 1918)

September

John Cage	(September 5, 1912)
Antonin Dvořák	(September 8, 1841)
Arnold Schoenberg	(September 13, 1874)
Charles Griffes	(September 17, 1884)
Dimitri Shostakovich	(September 25, 1906)
George Gershwin	(September 26, 1898)

October

Steve Reich	(October 3, 1936)
Camille Saint-Saëns	(October 9, 1835)
Giuseppe Verdi	(October 9 or 10, 1813)
Charles Ives	(October 20, 1874)
Franz Liszt	(October 22, 1811)
Georges Bizet	(October 25, 1838)
Domenico Scarlatti	(October 26, 1685)

November

Aleksandr Borodin	(November 12, 1833)
Aaron Copland	(November 14, 1900)
William Christopher Handy	(November 16, 1873)
Tommy Dorsey	(November 19, 1905)
Benjamin Britten	(November 22, 1913)
Scott Joplin	(November 24, 1868)

December

Jean Sibelius	(December 8, 1865)
Hector Berlioz	(December 11, 1803)
Ludwig van Beethoven	(December 17, 1770)
Giacomo Puccini	(December 23, 1858)

If composer does not appear, his month of birth is unknown.

Part Four

Resources

Appendix A

A Guide to Preschool Musical Instruction: Influences and Programs

The music education programs described below have had an important influence on the musical training of young children in America:

SHINICHI SUZUKI: TALENT EDUCATION PROGRAM

Suzuki's amazing success teaching violin to very young children led to the growth of the worldwide Talent Education Program, which is designed to teach instrumental performance even to the youngest students. His approach utilized and developed the acute hearing capacity of the child at an early age and the child's delight in the repetitive process. His teaching strategies also included these principles:

- For several weeks before the first lessons, parents daily play recorded pieces (including the first piece the child will learn). The child watches a lesson so that he can see and hear other children playing; then he is given his instrument.
- The "mother-tongue approach" is foundational. Suzuki taught music based on the way children learn their native language—first listening, copying, and then learning to read and write. The first pieces are learned by rote. "Ease comes with training," said Suzuki. "We simply have to train and educate our ability, that is to say to do the thing over and over again until it feels natural, simple and easy. That is the secret."[1]

- The training of the parent is in tandem with the training of the child. Parents attend each private lesson and monthly ensemble class and also learn to play the instrument themselves. The parent studies the manuals, practices daily with the child at home, and constantly encourages.
- After the child has learned to read, note reading is introduced. Every student follows the same sequence of materials so they have in common a repertory of music to play together in unison during monthly ensemble gatherings.
- Cooperation, not competition, is the motivation. Students at all levels play together, older students helping the younger.

Although the Suzuki approach began as a violin teaching method, its use has been adapted by teachers of other instruments such as cello, viola, flute, and harp.

YAMAHA MUSIC EDUCATION

This music education program was developed by educators commissioned by a manufacturing organization, Nippon Gakki/Yamaha Motors, and is concerned with the development and encouragement of popular as well as classical music. These are its characteristics:

- Great emphasis is placed on the development of creativity—not just giving all the attention to those who show special talent in this area, but encouraging creativity to stimulate the understanding and pleasure of all those who study music.
- The Yamaha method regards the study of music as a training in basic musicianship rather than the study of performance on a particular instrument. It is not a piano method.
- The four volumes of the Yamaha Primary Course are designed as a two-year basic musicianship program for children ages four to six.
- The Yamaha teaching philosophy emphasizes the importance of experience, especially that of the ear. The young student first learns to express rhythmic and melodic patterns through singing and whole-body activities. There is an introduction to the keyboard, but no attention is given to piano teaching or technique or tone production.
- All Yamaha programs involve group instruction, with a class size of eight to twelve children. Parents attend each class and participate in all activities so they can work with their children at home.

DALCROZE EURHYTHMICS

Devised by Emile Jaques-Dalcroze, a professor at the Geneva Conservatory of Music, this system teaches ear training and keyboard improvisation that stimulate the listening and creative abilities of students.

- Eurhythmics emphasizes rhythmic responses involving the use of the whole body. This is to stimulate awareness of the body's own natural movements and rhythms as well as to develop an ability to express various aspects of music such as melodic progression, dynamic change, and metric patterns by means of physical movement. Eurhythmics means "good rhythm" and has come to describe the Dalcroze method and any system teaching rhythm through movement.
- The Dalcroze training also involves training in *solfège* (voice practice in which scales are sung), ear training, and keyboard improvisation.
- Although most children's music programs at the time used regimented movements, Dalcroze techniques allowed and encouraged children to respond physically in natural, unrestricted ways. The student was not to imitate the movements of the teacher but use his imagination to improvise movement and sound.
- Dalcroze techniques were introduced in American schools from 1910 through the 1920s but never enjoyed widespread use. However, some teachers adapted Dalcroze techniques of rhythmic movements into their music programs.

CARL ORFF

The Orff Schulwerk approach was developed by Carl Orff, a German composer and educator. Orff was influenced by the ideas of Jaques-Dalcroze and believed in the importance of rhythm. Orff developed an approach to the teaching of rhythm and melody that grew out of the use of basic speech, singing, and movement patterns, and his work was published between 1930 and 1933. The Orff methods have profoundly influenced the principles and practice of elementary music education throughout the world.

Orff's philosophy was that music making was for everyone and that it should be started as early as possible. His method concentrated on giving children experiences on mallet-playing instruments. He produced a number of high-quality drums, percussion accessories, and other metallophones known as "Orff instruments" on which children could express rhythm and melody.

Orff's methods also include:

- an emphasis on the value of the folk song
- the use of speech patterns familiar through nursery rhymes and singing games to develop the child's understanding of meters and rhythms
- creativity through improvising
- bringing together natural rhythmic activity—clapping, running, skipping, stamping, snapping fingers, swaying—instrumental techniques, movement, aural training, and solo and choral singing

Orff's philosophy of music education had an impact throughout the United States, and Orff instruments have offered a way to combine instrumental performance with personal expression.

ZOLTÁN KODÁLY

Kodály's music education system was originally developed for the children of his native Hungary, but it became a model for the world. Kodály felt that as a child naturally learns his mother tongue before foreign languages, he should learn his musical mother tongue—the folk music of his own country. Here are some important Kodály principles:

- Good music is a necessity for everyone.
- Music education must begin early—usually at age three when the child enters nursery school—and must be taught as children learn: moving gradually from direct experiences to symbols.
- Music literacy, not just enjoyment or enrichment, is the ultimate goal of the Kodály method. With music literacy comes musical independence.
- It is the ear that must be trained, and that is best accomplished by beginning with the voice.
- Curriculum comes from the musical literature of the culture (folk music) and the musical development of children. Kodály felt that the simple forms of nursery songs and folk music were more appropriate for children because the language of folk music tends to be drawn from speech patterns familiar to children even before they enter school.
- Kodály's system uses a child-development sequence. For example, moving rhythms are more child-related than sustained ones. The quarter note is the child's walking pace, the eighth note, his running pace.
- Relative solfège provides a means of understanding what is heard.
- Early part work develops independence and interdependence.

- The aims of music training at the preschool level are to increase the child's love for music, help him sing in tune, begin to develop a sense of rhythm and beat, and begin to develop a sense of musical discrimination.
- Although the Kodály method focuses on singing, it also includes the use of instruments (after children have learned to read and write music as a result of singing experiences), excluding the piano.

Although the approach began in the 1920s, it did not have a wide influence in other parts of the world until the 1950s and in America in the 1960s. The Kodály method continues to influence music education.

A Parent's and Teacher's Guide to Music Resources

A wealth of good music resources are available, including books on music for parents and music-oriented books for children, audiotapes and videotapes, and computer software.

Many of these books can be found at your local public library or at online bookstores. If a book is not available, your library can get it through inter-library loan; just ask. In addition, most libraries are happy to order a book if you have all the publishing information, which is included here. Children's music books, like *Once Upon MacDonald's Farm* or *Music Lessons for Alex,* can be found in the children's section of the library. Other music books listed can be found in the nonfiction "music" category. The librarian can help you locate these books.

Some of the books, such as those on music history and composers, can be found in university or college music libraries. Many of these music libraries are happy to let people in the community use their resources.

Another good place to find many of the audiocassettes, CDs, and song-books on this list is at local music stores, good bookstores that have a children's section, Christian bookstores, and Web sites of music companies. Many general-interest bookstores have good selections of classical music at a low price.

The video chain stores have many videos of classical music performances, Broadway musicals, and other music resources. If you cannot find a resource listed here, I have included a list of selected publishers. They will send you free catalogs, and I have included toll-free numbers and Web sites, when available, for ordering resources.

Books: Composers

Ewen, David. *Composers of Today.* New York: H. W. Wilson Company, 1936. A comprehensive and critical guide of composers from most nations.

————. *Composers of Yesterday.* New York: H. W. Wilson Company, 1937. A critical guide to the most important composers of the past.

————. *The World of Great Composers.* Englewood Cliffs, N.J.: Prentice-Hall, 1962. Thirty-seven of the world's greatest composers are introduced first by a brief biography of each life, next by an informal, revealing portrait of the composer, then a critical appraisal of the composer's work, and finally, a statement by the composer himself in which he writes about his own work.

Kavanaugh, Patrick. *The Spiritual Lives of Great Composers.* Nashville: Sparrow Press, 1992. Kavanaugh has selected twelve famous composers and researched their spiritual beliefs from their personal letters, journals, and colorful, contemporary accounts. Included are Handel, Bach, Haydn, Mozart, Beethoven, Schubert, Mendelssohn, Liszt, Wagner, Dvořák, Ives, and Stravinsky.

Slonimsky, Nicolas. *Baker's Biographical Dictionary of Musicians.* 8th ed. New York: Schirmer Books, 1991. A book of approximately two thousand pages with short biographies of almost every major and minor composer/musician, arranged in alphabetical order.

Books: Dictionaries

Ammer, Christine. *Harper's Dictionary of Music.* New York: Barnes & Noble, 1972. A paperback dictionary, less detailed than the *Harvard Dictionary of Music* but excellent.

Apel, Willi. *Harvard Dictionary of Music.* Cambridge: Harvard University Press, 1987. A comprehensive dictionary containing thorough definitions on practically every aspect of classical music.

Headington, Christopher. *Illustrated Dictionary of Music.* New York: Harper & Row, 1980. A concise dictionary of music terms.

Books: General Music

Headington, Christopher. *History of Western Music*. New York: Schirmer
    Books, 1976. A concise history and criticism of music.
Hoffer, Charles R. *The Understanding of Music*. Belmont, Calif.: Wadsworth
    Publishing, 1968. Guide to live performance for the understanding of
    music. Illustrated.
Machlis, Joseph. *The Enjoyment of Music*. 5th ed. New York: Norton and
    Company, 1984. A very readable survey of Western art music. Record-
    ings, tapes, and CDs are available, containing performances of featured
    works by a wide variety of composers.
Sadie, Stanley. *Brief Guide to Music*. 2d ed. Englewood Cliffs, N.J.: Prentice-
    Hall, 1987. Another excellent survey of Western art music. Recordings,
    tapes, and compact discs are available containing featured performances
    by a wide variety of composers.
Stolba, K. Marie. *The Development of Western Music: A History*. Dubuque,
    Iowa: Wm. C. Brown, 1990. A very comprehensive history of music.
    Available along with the main book are anthologies, recordings, tapes,
    and compact discs of the music, videotapes, and transparencies.
Ulrich, Homer. *Music: A Design for Listening*. 3d ed. New York: Harcourt,
    Brace and World, 1970. A book designed to guide any listener in his
    search for musical enjoyment and understanding.

Books: Instruments

Buchner, Alexander. *Musical Instruments Through the Ages*. Translated by
    Borek Vancura. New York: Crown, 1976.
Diagram Group. *Musical Instruments of the World*. New York: Paddington
    Press, 1976. An illustrated encyclopedia and dictionary.
Headington, Christopher. *The Orchestra and Its Instruments*. New York:
    Harper & Row, 1965. Illustrations and descriptions of the instruments
    of the orchestra.
Marcuse, Sibl. *Musical Instruments: A Comprehensive Dictionary*. New York:
    Norton and Company, 1975. A complete, authoritative encyclopedia
    of instruments throughout the world; paperback, dictionary format.
Walther, Tom. *Make My Music*. New York: Little, Brown, 1981. A great
    source for directions on making a variety of instruments such as the
    glockenspiel.

Wiseman, Ann. *Making Musical Things*. New York: Scribner, 1979.
A great book with instructions for making simple instruments, such
as a Native-American rain stick, mainly with common household
items.

Books: Piano Music/History

Friskin, James, and Irwin Freundlich. *Music for the Piano*. New York: Dover
Publications, 1973. A paperback book listing compositions written by
leading composers for early keyboards and the piano. Gradings, descriptions, and publishers are listed. Also contains listings of piano ensemble
music and music for piano and orchestra.

Gillespie, John. *Five Centuries of Keyboard Music*. New York: Dover Publications, 1965. A historical survey of music for the harpsichord and piano.
Illustrations included.

Hinson, Maurice. *Guide to the Pianist's Repertoire*. Bloomington: Indiana
University Press, 1987. Listings of the representative works of each composer in alphabetical order, graded, including bibliographic entries, and
listings of periodicals and editions.

Books: Twentieth-Century Music

Salzman, Eric. *Twentieth Century Music: An Introduction*. 2d ed. Englewood
Cliffs, N.J.: Prentice-Hall, 1967. One of the concise yet comprehensive
and authoritative paperbacks from the music history series published by
Prentice-Hall. The several volumes cover music from the medieval world
up to the late twentieth century.

Simms, Bryan R. *Music of the Twentieth Century*. New York: Schirmer
Books, 1986. This book contains examples of twentieth-century music
with brief bibliography and discography listings for each piece. Of special interest are the unusual notations characteristic of much of the
music of the twentieth century.

Books: For Children

Adams, Pat. *There Was an Old Lady Who Swallowed a Fly*. Singapore: Child's
Play (International), 1990. A great book for children, featuring this
familiar song. Excellent illustrations.

Arnold, Caroline. *Music Lessons for Alex.* New York: Clarion Books, 1983. This book shows the step-by-step process involved in learning to play a musical instrument through the story and photographs of Alex, from the very beginning of the first violin lesson to her first recital a year later. Inspiring for any child who wants to learn to play an instrument.

Feierabend, John. *Music for Little People.* New York: Boosey & Hawkes, 1989. Book and audiocassette set with fifty playful activities for preschool and early elementary children. This collection of traditional folk songs and rhymes is suitable for three- to seven-year-olds.

————. *Music for Very Little People.* New York: Boosey & Hawkes, 1986. Fifty playful activities for infants and toddlers to share with adults. This collection of traditional folk songs and rhymes won the Paul Revere Award for Best Educational Children's Folio.

Gammell, Stephen. *Once Upon MacDonald's Farm.* New York: Aladdin Books, 1981. This clever book for children has a revised story about Old MacDonald and can be used in conjunction with the familiar folk song. Gammell is the illustrator of several other music-related books, including *Waiting to Waltz* (Cynthia Rylant), *The Old Banjo* (Dennis Haseley), and *The Song and Dance Man* (Karen Ackerman).

Hurd, Thacher. *Mama Don't Allow.* New York: Harper & Row, 1984. A clever story for children about some animals who formed a band that was appreciated only by the alligators in the swamp and how they escaped. Used with the song "Mama Don't Allow," which is noted in the back of the book.

Kovalski, Maryann. *The Wheels on the Bus.* New York: Little, Brown, 1987. A very clever book for children based on the traditional song with the same name; book can be used in conjunction with the song.

Peek, Merle. *Mary Wore Her Red Dress.* New York: Clarion Books, 1985. This book for children could be a fun point of departure for parents and teachers, using the familiar folk tune, which is noted in the back of the book.

Raffi. *Five Little Ducks; One Light, One Sun; Shake My Sillies Out* (plus other titles). New York: Crown, 1987. Raffi has been known for years as Canada's most successful children's recording artist. His live performances, albums, songbooks, and concert video have made him one of North America's premier children's entertainers. The above-mentioned books are just some of a series for children called Songs to Read. Songs are noted in the back of each book.

Westcott, Nadine Barnard. *Peanut Butter and Jelly*. New York: Dutton Children's Books, 1987. A favorite play rhyme takes on super-duper proportions as two children create a table-sized sandwich from scratch. Hand and body actions are included in the back of the book.

Zemach, Harve, and Margot Zemach. *Mommy, Buy Me a China Doll*. New York: Farrar, Straus, & Giroux, 1989. This book for children is adapted from the Ozark children's song with the same name. Excerpts from the song can be sung throughout the story.

Books: For Parents, Teachers, and the Mature Child

Bayless, Kathleen M., and Marjorie E. Ramsey. *Music: A Way of Life for the Young Child*. 4th ed. New York: Macmillan, 1991. Contains music, text, and activities for children from infancy through five years, including suggested activities for children through the day and for children with special needs, along with highlights of a child's musical heritage.

Ben-Tovim, Atarah, and Douglas Boyd. *The Right Instrument for Your Child: A Practical Guide for Parents and Teachers*. New York: Morrow, 1985. Advice for parents on finding just the right instrument for your child's physical, mental, and personality makeup, with a series of simple questions to help you determine the best possibilities.

Bloom, Benjamin. *Developing Talent in Young People*. New York: Ballantine Books, 1985. Explores in detail each of the crucial stages of talent development and offers parents and teachers important new insights into this fascinating subject.

Campbell, Don. *The Mozart Effect for Children*. New York: Morrow, 2000. This book explores how to awaken a child's mind, health, and creativity with music. An excellent resource on infant and child development and music.

DeMoss, Robert G., Jr. *Learn to Discern*. Grand Rapids: Zondervan, 1992.

Edwards, Linda Carol. *Affective Development and the Creative Arts*. Columbus, Ohio: Merrill, 1990. A very good book emphasizing music, drama, art, and literature for the young child. Has a special section on the basic stages of early musical development.

Evans, Rob. *Sing-along Songbooks*. Mobile, Ala.: Integrity Music, 1992. Donut Man series books, containing more than sixty songs of praise and worship especially suited for kids. Includes thirteen Christmas songs.

Special attention is given to make them easy to sing and play. Audio-cassettes available.

Ewen, David. *Songs of America*. Glenview, Ill.: Greenwood Press, 1978. A collection of distinctly American songs, along with related comments.

Fowke, Edith. *Ring Around the Moon*. Dallas, Tex.: Music in Motion, 1987. This book contains two hundred songs, tongue twisters, riddles, rhymes, rounds, animal songs, endless songs, charms, and answer-back songs for children, drawn entirely from the oral tradition of North America. Songs are noted and range from silly to sentimental.

Fox, Donna Brink. "Music, Development, and the Young Child." *Music Educator Journal* 77, no. 5, January 1991. An excellent article dealing with very early (prenatal) music responses and their significance in a child's musical development.

Goode, Diane. *American Folk Tales and Songs*. New York: Dutton, 1989. This book is a collection of tales and songs for reading, for telling, and for singing (notation included). All come out of America's rich oral tradition, from the many regions and ethnic groups that make up this country. Good resource for teachers and parents and a fine collection for the older child.

Herrold, Rebecca M. *New Approaches to Elementary Classroom Music*. 2d ed. Englewood Cliffs, N.J.: Prentice-Hall, 1991. An excellent source for resources and materials for music, including a list of software suppliers and specific music software packages and the computers they work with.

Kingswriter, Doug, and Debbie Kingswriter. *God's Plan of Salvation*. Irving, Tex.: Word Music, 1990. A G. T. and the Halo Express series musical for kids, dedicated to hiding God's Word in the hearts of children.

Kirkland, Terry, and Richard Ham. *Pocket Book of Camping Songs*. Nashville: Broadman, 1977. Contains a collection of hymns and songs designed especially for day camps, retreats, special summer activities, or any time you want to draw a youngster's attention to God and his great out-of-doors.

———. *Pocket Book of Fun Songs*. Nashville: Broadman, 1977. Contains songs filled with fun and action: rounds, canons, and nonsense verses just for the fun of singing. Every song has chord markings for guitar, ukulele, and piano; most of the songs may also be played on the autoharp.

———. *Pocket Book of Rounds*. Nashville: Broadman, 1977. Contains new and old rounds good for any age, anytime, and anywhere you have a group of people together and the opportunity to sing.

Peery, J. Craig, and Irene W. Peery, eds. *Music and Child Development.* New York: Springer-Verlag, 1987. This book covers a variety of subjects, including the role of music in child development, the development of musical abilities, the relationship of music and language skills, as well as musical experiences throughout the various ages of children from infancy through the classroom years.

Schaeffer, Edith. *Forever Music: A Tribute to the Gift of Creativity.* Grand Rapids, Mich.: Baker, 1986. The story of how the gift of a grand piano began a new page in Edith Schaeffer's life following the death of her husband, Francis. She draws lessons on life and creativity from the history and making of a piano at Steinway and Sons and from her visits with Franz Mohr, master piano technician.

Schafer, R. Murray. *Creative Music Education.* New York: Schirmer Books, 1976. A book for music teachers that deals with five principal issues of music education: creativity, ear training, the sound scape, works and music, and music in relation to other arts. It is not a book that says, "Do it this way." It only says, "I did it this way." The author's approach to the above issues is quite unusual and worth investigating.

Shaw, Gordon L. *Keeping Mozart in Mind.* San Diego: Academic Press, 1999. A fascinating book on classical music's effect on children's brain development by the pioneer who first did the research on this subject.

Smith, Jane Stuart, and Betty Carlson. *A Gift of Music: Great Composers and Their Influence.* Wheaton, Ill.: Good News, 1978. Stories of great composers and their influence in the development of music.

Sommer, Elyse. *The Kid's World Almanac of Music from Rock to Bach.* New York: Pharos Books, 1992. Good reference book.

Storms, Jerry. *101 Music Games for Children.* Alameda, Calif.: Hunter House, 1995. Includes many creative ideas for musical games that include singing, moving, and listening.

Suzuki, Shinichi. *Nurtured by Love: A New Approach to Education.* Athens, Ohio: Ability Development Press, 1987. Suzuki's ideals and ideas of his Talent Education Program. Excellent, practical, and very interesting.

Wilson, Frank. *Tone Deaf and All Thumbs? An Invitation to Music-Making for Late Bloomers and Non Prodigies.* New York: Viking-Penguin, 1986. Written by a brain surgeon who learned piano later in life.

Yolen, Jane. *The Lullaby Songbook.* New York: Harcourt-Brace, 1986. A collection of lullabies.

Magazines: For Children

Piano Explorer. Published by The Instrumentalist, 200 Northfield Rd., Northfield, IL 60093; 847-446-5000. An excellent magazine for children, containing general music information, games, puzzles, and music to play. Not just for pianists and very reasonably priced. The company also publishes *The Instrumentalist* for band and orchestra directors and students aspiring to be directors and *The Flute* for students of the flute.

AUDIO RESOURCES

There are hundreds of audiocassettes available, and it is not possible to list them all in this section. Hopefully, the few that are highlighted will lead you to others.

Classical

Anthologies of music that have music scores and/or audiocassettes and/or CDs are included in the section "Books: General Music." Please check the listings for Joseph Machlis *(The Enjoyment of Music),* Stanley Sadie *(Brief Guide to Music),* and K. Marie Stolba *(The Development of Western Music: A History).*

Beethoven Lives Upstairs, by Sue Hammond. Excerpts of Beethoven's compositions plus a riveting narrative that combine for an interesting story and musical education. Winner of the Notable Children's Recording Awards and the 1990 Juno Award for Best Children's Recording. Teacher's guide available. Included in Month 6: Beethoven of "Classics Month-by-Month."

Daydreams and Lullabies. A delightful celebration of classical music and children's poems featuring all the classical kids' composers from Mozart to Vivaldi. Available from Music for Little People.

Fiedler's Favorites for Children contains familiar melodies arranged to be fun and inviting to children's ears; includes "Sabre Dance," selections from *The Nutcracker Suite,* "Chim-Chim-Cher-ee," and others. Also, *More Fiedler's Favorites for Children* offers other familiar selections, including "Carnival of the Animals," "Dance of the Sugar Plum Fairy," and "Bugler's Holiday." Available on audiocassette and performed by Arthur Fiedler and the Boston Pops.

G'morning Johann, by Ric Louchard. Classical piano solos for morning time. Greet the new day with dreamy tranquil moments, gently leading to cheerful allegro jubilation. Available from Music for Little People.

G'morning Wolfgang, by Ric Louchard. Classical piano solos and natural lullabies, these twelve gentle pieces are played just as they were written by Mozart, Beethoven, Bach, Satie, and Schumann. Available from Music for Little People.

Hush, by Bobby McFerrin and Yo-Yo Ma. Features virtuoso performances by award-winning vocalist Bobby McFerrin and famed cellist Yo-Yo Ma. Works by Bach, Vivaldi, Rachmaninoff, and others are done in a style that often surprises and unfailingly delights. Includes "Flight of the Bumblebee," "Ave Maria," "Hoedown!" and ten more. Available in audiocassette and CD from Columbia Records.

Mr. Bach Comes to Call, by Sue Hammond. Eight-year-old Elizabeth is practicing Bach's Minuet in G when the composer appears with his magic orchestra and chair and tells of his life and music. Winner of the Notable Children's Recording Award, 1989 Juno Award nomination for Best Children's Recording, and 1989 Parents' Choice Award. Teacher's guide available. Included in Month 2: Bach of "Classics Month-by-Month."

Mozart's Magic Fantasy, by Sue Hammond. This tape is based on Mozart's opera, *The Magic Flute.* The story involves a child, Sarah, who must confront the forces of good and evil. In the end, Sarah is ready to return to her own world and "step out into the music" of Mozart's great overture. This work received the 1991 Juno Award for Best Children's Recording. Teacher's guide available. Included in Month 5: Mozart of "Classics Month-by-Month."

The Orchestra, by Mark Rubin and Alan Daniel. Book and tape, read by Peter Ustinov and performed by the Toronto Philharmonic Orchestra. A great introduction to the instruments of the orchestra. Available in video, audiocassette, CD, or book and tape from Firefly Books, Buffalo, New York.

Peter and the Wolf. Available in several versions, this music-story by Prokofiev provides a natural and fun way to introduce children to classical music. Available on audiocassette or CD.

The Top 100 Masterpieces of Classical Music. Favorites from Bach, Mozart, Beethoven, Tchaikovsky, and others performed by the world's best orchestras and musicians. Available from Friendship House.

Vivaldi's Ring of Mystery, by Sue Hammond. The story revolves around a child who enters Vivaldi's life while he is the music director at an orphanage in Venice. Katrina is curious about her origins, and with the help of Giovanni, the gondolier, and Vivaldi, she finds her answer. There are over two dozen examples of Vivaldi's music, including the *Four Seasons.* Teacher's guide available. Included in Month 1: Vivaldi of "Classics Month-by-Month."

A Young Musician's Classical Library. Eighteen cassettes explore the lives and music of great composers. Available from Friendship House (see Publishers/Distributors of Materials).

Young Person's Guide to the Orchestra, by Benjamin Britten. Britten has taken a theme by Henry Purcell and given each instrument of the orchestra an opportunity to play it alone in a characteristic setting, then together. See Month 4: Haydn in "Classics Month-by-Month."

Music Resources for Babies and Young Children

With the explosion of research on the benefits of classical music in early childhood has come a wealth of new music CDs, videos, and materials. Here is a sampling:

Baby Genius Video Collection, including *Mozart and Friends* and *Mozart and Friends Sleepytime.* Capitalizing on the Mozart Effect, these videos are engaging and age-appropriate ways to introduce classical music to your baby and preschooler. Ages birth to forty-eight months. For more information contact www.babygenius.com.

Baby Mozart: Musical Experiences to Stimulate and Delight Your Baby. This video comes with a free *Baby Mozart CD. The Baby Mozart Concert for Little Ears* offers stimulating classics for babies. Both products are for children one month to three years and are from the Baby Einstein Company, www.babyeinstein.com, 800-793-1454. Also available at most learning stores.

Baby Music School: Classical. This package from the Baby School Company, containing a video, audiocassettes, and rhythm ball, introduces classical music with a hands-on approach to infants and preschoolers six months to four years. Available in learning stores.

Baby's Smart Start: Stimulating Your Child with Images and Classical Music. This video comes with a free parents' guide and is for children ages three months to three years. Available through www.babyscapes.com or 888-441-KIDS.

Embryonics Learning System from Womb to Classroom. This package includes creative classical music video and audio resources for children ages one year and up. Call Munchkin at 800-344-2229 or visit their Web site at www.munchkininc.com.

Horace Hopper's Music Adventures Piano Starter Kit for Preschoolers and Moms. This kit contains a keyboard for kids, three CDs, an illustrated storybook, twelve musical adventures, and twenty-three songs and sound effects. For kids ages three to five years. Available through www.PreschoolMusic.com or 888-291-4174.

John Tesh Presents Classical Music for Babies (and Their Moms). A wonderful CD for babies available through your local bookstore or music store.

Little Explorers Volumes 1 and 2: Adventures in Art, Music, and Dance are lively videos that encourage music and movement and integrate the arts in an imaginative way for children ages birth to four years. From Cassidy Video Production, 888-71-VIDEO, www.little-explorers.com.

Music Blocks: Music for Your Child's Mind. Each block in this package plays a different phrase of Mozart's music and gives kids an easy way to make music all on their own. Available through www.neurosmith.com.

Christian Music Resources

A Capella Kids. This Grammy-winning children's recording brings together ten superb renditions of children's Sunday school classics, praise songs, and contemporary Christian hits, sung by the Kids' Praise kids. Children and adults alike will enjoy this unique recording. Available from Benson Music Group

And the Angels Sing. Boston Museum of Fine Arts commissioned this Baroque recording of strings, harp, brass, harpsichord, and other instruments. Available from Baker Book House.

Arky's Favorite Toddler Tales, Tunes, and Poems. A full-length audiocassette featuring songs, stories, poems, and sound effects developed just for toddlers. Biblical and family values are taught in this most entertaining release. Available from Benson Music Group.

Barry Bear's Very Best Bedtime Bible Stories, vols. 1 and 2. Features Bible stories and lullabies for children. Comes with book. Both cassette and video available from Brentwood Music.

Christmas Messiah for Young Voices, arranged by Timothy W. Sharp and James Michael. Contains many of the famous choruses, recitatives, and arias from Handel's *Messiah,* arranged for two-part children's voices. Soundtrack, audition pack, and stereo audiocassette available, as well as the song book with a simplified piano accompaniment. Available from Integra Music.

The Donut Man. See "Evans, Rob" under the section "Books: For Parents, Teachers, and the Mature Child," for information on books and tapes presented by The Donut Man. Evans is worship leader on several listening cassettes for children. The sing-along songbook is helpful for families who enjoy Hosanna Praise Music. Available from Integrity Music.

Good Buddies, by Mary Rice Hopkins. On this particular recording, Hopkins focuses on teaching children how to build self-esteem and good relationships with others. *Good Buddies* is about friendships, cooperation, growth, obedience, and forgiveness. Available from Benson Music Group.

G. T. and the Halo Express. Collections of Scripture songs. Each tape teaches ten Scripture verses. Available from Word, Inc.

Hide 'Em in Your Heart Lullabies, Hide 'Em in Your Heart Praise and Worship, Hide 'Em in Your Heart, vols. 1 and 2. Steve Green is accompanied by a children's choir in singing these wonderfully written Scripture songs for both parents and children. Available from Sparrow Corporation.

Hymns Triumphant, parts 1 and 2, performed by the London Philharmonic Choir and the National Philharmonic Orchestra. Many favorite beautifully performed hymns that will be inspirational, worshipful, and uplifting. Available from Sparrow Records, Inc.

Hymnworks, vols. 1 and 2, by Linda McKechnie. Familiar classical themes are woven into beloved hymns. Full orchestra with solo piano.

I Love You. This tape includes many songs of blessing designed for infants. Available from Integrity Music.

Kids Sing Praise, vols. 1-3. Action songs of praise, Scripture, and sing-along fun for children. Both cassette and video available. Split track for sing-along or group performance. Available from Brentwood Music.

Lighthouse, by Mary Rice Hopkins. This recording takes children on a musical roller-coaster ride that at times is tender and other times ticklish. Children will learn they are to be the salt of the earth and the light of the world. There is an international flavor to this recording that calls us all to live in unity. Available from Benson Music Group.

The Master Musician, by John Michael Talbot. An innovative music story-telling tape that shares a metaphor about God, the Master Musician, fashioning us as his instruments and our playing together in the Symphony of Life. Available from Sparrow Records, Inc.

Once Upon an Orchestra. This is the musical story of Symphonyville, where instruments live, work, and play. It brings the sound and personality of the instruments to life for your child. It tells the story of Sydney Saxophone, who feels he doesn't fit into the orchestra but learns to use his talents to make beautiful music for the Creator—and it communicates that God has uniquely created each child and has special plans for her too. The original score includes selections from Bach, Beethoven, and other classical themes. It also comes with a poster that shows where each instrument is located in the orchestra. Available from Brentwood Music.

The Singing Bible. Contains fifty original sing-along songs that set Scripture to music. Published by Focus on the Family Heritage Builders, ages seven and under. Available at Christian bookstores or through Focus on the Family: 800-AFAMILY, www.fotf.org.

Sing, Stretch & Play and *Big Songs for Little Kids: I Feel Like Dancing.* These CDs and videos combine movement and music—and lots of fun! Available from Brentwood Kids Video, www.brentwoodrecords.com.

Sleep Sound in Jesus and *Come to the Cradle* by Michael Card. Lovely, high-quality music for babies and young children, a bestseller. Available from Sparrow Records, Inc.

Smoky Mountain Kids. Contains twenty-two action-filled songs featuring handmade instruments for sing-along. Both cassette and video available. Split track for group performance. Available from Brentwood Music.

Tiny Tot Pwaise, vols. 1-6. This is some of the first Christian children's music made especially for toddlers. The melodies are fun and easy to sing and understand for children twelve months to four years old. Available from Benson Music Group.

The "25" Series. *25 Hymns Kids Love to Sing, 25 Sunday School Songs Kids Love to Sing, 25 Bible Action Songs Kids Love to Sing,* and four other sing-along CDs. Available from Sparrow Records, Inc.

The Word & Song Bible, published by Lifeway Christian Resources, available in bookstores. The Bible plus audio pack of five CDs for children of all ages.

Traditional/Folk/Lullabies

American Folksongs for Children, by Mike and Peggy Seeger. This extensive collection of ninety-four tunes includes just about every family folk song we've ever heard. America's foremost folk family plays guitar, banjo, mandolin, pan pipes, concertina, fiddle, and more. Companion book includes words and music to all these favorite folk songs, plus fun activities and interesting information. Two audiocassettes, two CDs available from Music for Little People.

Best of Burl's for Boys and Girls, by Burl Ives. Includes "I Know an Old Lady, "Polly Wolly Doodle," "Aunt Rhody," "The Man on the Flying Trapeze," "Big Rock Candy Mountain," and twelve more. Available from Music for Little People.

A Child's Celebration of Showtunes. Contains some of the best children's music from shows of the past fifty years, including Mary Martin singing "I Won't Grow Up" and "I'm Flying" from *Peter Pan,* Dick Van Dyke singing "Put on a Happy Face" from *Bye Bye Birdie,* and many others. Available from Music for Little People.

A Child's Celebration of Song. Contains some of the best children's music of the past fifty years. Includes The Doobie Brothers singing "Wynken, Blynken and Nod," Judy Garland singing "Over the Rainbow," Pete Seeger singing "This Old Man," and many other artists and songs. Available from Music for Little People.

For Kids and Other People: Horse Sense. The American cowboy will always fascinate children and grownups too. Performing around the world, Justin and Ted breathe new life into songs born on the great trail drives of the 1800s. Features guitar, fiddle, mandolin, and banjo. Includes "Git Along Little Dogies," "Red River Valley," "Old Chisholm Trail," and others. Available from Music for Little People.

Little White Duck, by Burl Ives. This great-granddaddy to folk music inspired a whole generation with his style and spirit. Includes "Little White Duck," "The Little Engine That Could," "Mr. Froggie Went A-Courtin'," "Fooba Wooba John," "The Donut Song," and ten more. Available from Music for Little People.

Music for Little People, by John Feierabend. Book and cassette tape set with fifty playful activities for preschool and early elementary children. This collection of traditional folk songs and rhymes is suited to three- to seven-year-olds. Available from First Steps in Music.

Music for Very Little People, by John Feierabend. Fifty playful activities for infants and toddlers to share with adults. This collection of traditional folk songs and rhymes won the Paul Revere Award for Best Educational Children's Folio. Available from First Steps in Music.

Peter, Paul and Mommy, by Peter, Paul and Mary. Contains favorites like "Puff, the Magic Dragon," "I Have a Song to Sing," and many more. Available from Warner Bros.

Rory's Little Broadway, by Rory. A collection of favorite accompanied Broadway songs. Great for sing-along. Available from Sony Kids Music.

Singable Songs, More Singable Songs, Baby Beluga, Corner Grocery Store, Rise and Shine, by Raffi. See "Books: for Children" for more information about Raffi. Raffi sings a variety of folk songs, nursery rhymes, and other songs for children. Available from A&M Records, Shoreline label.

VIDEOCASSETTES

Many videos of classical music performances are available from the larger video-store chains.

General

Music and Early Childhood. Thirty-minute documentary gives parents and educators information about musical child development from birth through the early elementary years. Featuring the work of John Feierabend and the Connecticut Center for Early Childhood Education and Music and Movement. Available from First Steps in Music, Inc.

Classical

Ballet on Video. Among others are *The Little Humpbacked Horse, Cinderella Ballet,* and *L'enfant et les sortilèges.* Stories told through ballet, especially accessible to children. Available from Kulture Video.

Music on Video. A wide variety of excellent music videos on the lives of composers, musical instruments, performances, history, and technology in music. On the expensive side, but worth checking. Call for a brochure and see if perhaps your library will order for you. (Contact Films for the Humanities and Sciences, P.O. Box 2053, Princeton, NJ 08543-2053, 800-257-5126, 609-452-1128.)

The Orchestra, by Mark Rubin and Alan Daniel. Book and tape, read by
Peter Ustinov and performed by the Toronto Philharmonic Orchestra. A
great introduction to the instruments of the orchestra.

Christian/Traditional

Contact the publishers listed in the section Publishers of Materials for a listing
of their products.

Amazing Grace (Provident Bookstores, 616 Walnut Avenue, Scottsdale, PA
15683-1999, 412-887-8500). Documentary that shares the story
behind "Amazing Grace," possibly the most popular song in the English
language. This remarkable video explores the song's history through the
people who have sung it.

Hollywood film classics such as *Doctor Doolittle, Annie, Peter Pan, The Sound
of Music, Mary Poppins, The Wizard of Oz, The Red Balloon, Heidi,* and
Rebecca of Sunnybrook Farm are available.

Mother Goose Goes to School. An exciting adventure for preschoolers. Sing-
along songs about starting the day, science and discovery, the wonder of
God's world, and the fun of learning. Available from Brentwood Kids
Co., Brentwood Music.

Tiny Tot Pwaise. This is among the first video series specifically designed for
toddlers. Children age fourteen months will be delighted with Arky the
Ark and his friends. Arky represents sound biblical and wholesome
values for families with small children. The videos feature electronic
animation and live-action sequences with toddlers, places, and animals.
Available from Benson Music Group.

Wee Sing Videos. This immensely popular series has sold millions of records
and tapes. Full of favorite songs and rhymes, these sparkling bright one-
hour videos entrance and capture a child's imagination. Songbook
included. Titles include "Marvelous Musical Mansion," "Wee Sing
Together," "Wee Sing in Sillyville," and "Grandpa's Magical Toys." Available from Music for Little People.

SELECTED PUBLISHERS/DISTRIBUTORS OF MATERIALS

Most of the publishers and distributors listed below have free catalogs of their
products. For a more complete list, please consult their catalogs or Web sites.

Brentwood-Benson Music Group. 741 Cool Springs Blvd., Franklin, TN
30767. Phone: 800-444-4012. A variety of Christian music for children,
especially in their Kids Sing Praise series. www.Brentwood-bensonmusic.
com.

Chinaberry Book Service. 2780 Via Orange Way, Suite B, Spring Valley, CA
91978. Phone: 800-776-2242. Specializes in books and music for children and families. www.Isabellacatalog.com.

Classical Kids. Distributed through Children's Bookstore Distribution.
Phone: 416-653-1868 or www.childrensgroup.com. (*Mr. Bach Comes to
Call, Mozart's Magic Fantasy, Beethoven Lives Upstairs, Tchaikovsky Visits
America, Mad About Kids Classics,* and other classical composer CDs and
videos.)

Focus on the Family. 8605 Explorer Drive, Colorado Springs, CO 80920.
Phone: 800-AFAMILY or 719-531-3400. www.Fotf.org. Many books,
cassettes, CDs, and videos available for parents, teens, and children. In
addition, their Heritage Builders resources include "The Singing Bible"
and other great materials.

Friendship House. 29313 Clemens Road, #2-G, P.O. Box 450978, Cleve-
land, OH 44145-0623. Phone: 440-871-8040.
www.friendshiphouse.com. Excellent resource for ordering music games,
audiocassettes, CDs, videos, and gifts.

Integrity Music. Division of Church Resource Division. 1000 Cody Road,
Mobile, AL 36695. Phone: 800-239-7000. Christian music with a special emphasis on children's resources. www.Integritymusic.com.

Lillenas Publishing Company. Box 419527, Kansas City, MO 64141.
Phone: 800-877-0700. Huge selection of music related to kids, including musicals (seasonal and nonseasonal), graded songbooks and recordings for young voices, Scripture songs, graded piano, and much more.
www.Lillenasmusic.com or www.nph.com.

MMB Music, Inc. Contemporary Arts Bldg. 3526 Washington Avenue,
Saint Louis, MO 63103-1019. Phone: 314-531-9635. A combined creative arts therapy and general music education publisher of materials
that include music dramas for children, music for creative expression,
music therapy, and music for developing speech and language skills in
children (with guidebook for parents and therapists). Huge selection of
materials. www.Mmbmusic.com.

Music for Little People. Box 747 Greenland, NH 03840. Phone: 800-409-
2457. This company is committed to finding products for their music

catalog that are helpful to parents, families, and teachers in creating a better world for children. Products include books, instruments, videos, CDs, audiocassettes, and more. Large variety of products. www.Mflp.com.

Music in Motion. P.O. Box 869231, Plano, TX 76086-9231. Phone: 800-445-0649. www.Musicmotion.com.

Provident Music Distribution. 741 Cool Springs Blvd., Franklin, TN 37067. Phone: 800-333-9000; Fax: 615-373-0386. Providentmusic.com. Many music items for children, but their Bible story series is of special interest.

RESOURCES FOR CHILDREN TO ENCOURAGE MUSICAL SKILLS AND MOVEMENT

Sparrow Corporation. P.O. Box 5085, Brentwood, TN 37024. Phone: 615-371-6800. A wide variety of Scripture songs and other children's music available. www.Emicmg.com.

Word Entertainment. 3319 West End Avenue, Suite 200, Nashville, TN 37203. Phone: 800-876-9673. Large selection of materials for kids, including music, CDs, and audiocassettes, Christmas music, musicals/songbooks, choral collections, piano music, and curriculum. www.Wordmusic.com.

Youth Specialties. P.O. Box 668, Holmes, PA 19043. Phone: 800-776-8008. General resources for teaching, art, games, discussions, and music with a Christian emphasis. www.Youthspecialties.com.

Notes

Foreword

1. Charlie Peacock, *At the Crossroads: An Insider's Look at the Past, Present, and Future of Contemporary Christian Music* (Nashville: Broadman & Holman, 1999), 85.

Chapter Two: The Joys and Benefits of Music Making

1. John Feierabend, "Music in Early Childhood," *Symposium on Early Childhood Arts Education,* July-August 1990, 15-20.
2. From interviews with Drs. John Feierabend and Edwin Gordon.
3. Feierabend, "Music in Early Childhood," 15-20.
4. From an interview with Gordon Shaw, professor, University of California at Irvine.
5. From "Music & Your Child," a message delivered at the American Music Conference, 1988.
6. David M. Mazie, "Music's Surprising Power to Heal," *Readers Digest,* August 1992, 173-8.
7. Mazie, "Music's Surprising Power to Heal," 175.
8. Mazie, "Music's Surprising Power to Heal," 175.
9. Al Menconi, with Dave Hart, *Today's Music: A Window to Your Child's Soul* (Elgin, Ill.: David C. Cook, 1990), 153.
10. Menconi with Hart, *Today's Music,* adapted from 154.

Chapter Four: Your Child's Musical Development

1. Sally Rogers, quoted in Donna Brink Fox, "Music, Development, and the Young Child," *Music Educator's Journal* (January 1991): 45.
2. Suzuki's book, *Nurtured by Love: A New Approach to Education,* outlines his educational philosophy and principles for successful early musical development.
3. From Edwin E. Gordon and Carl E. Seashore, *The Nature and Description of Developmental and Stabilized Music Aptitude: Implications for Music Learning* (Chicago: GLA Publishers, 1988).

4. Donna Brink Fox, "Music, Development, and the Young Child," *Music Educator's Journal* (January 1991): 43.

5. Fox, "Music, Development, and the Young Child," 43.

6. Fox, "Music, Development, and the Young Child," 44.

7. Fox, "Music, Development, and the Young Child," 46.

8. Kathleen Cushman, "Don't Let the Singing Stop," *Reader's Digest,* January 1993, 167.

9. Linda Carol Edwards, *Active Development and the Creative Arts* (Columbus, Ohio: Merrill, Macmillan, 1990), 36.

10. Edwards, *Active Development,* 36.

11. See appendix B.

12. If you don't know any finger-play songs, see *Wee Sing Children's Songs & Fingerplays* (Price/Stern/Sloan record, audiocassette) or *Baby's First Finger Rhymes* by Maida Silverman (Grossett & Dunlap, 1987).

13. Jane Healey, *Your Child's Growing Mind* (New York: Doubleday, 1987), 330.

14. Edwards, *Active Development,* 36.

15. See appendix A for an explanation of each of these musical education programs.

16. Healey, *Your Child's Growing Mind,* 332.

17. Linda Kelley and Brian Sutton-Smith, "A Study of Infant Musical Productivity," in J. Craig Peery, *Music and Child Development* (New York: Springer-Verlag, 1987), 35-53.

18. Edwards, *Active Development,* 37, and Marguerite Miller, *Know Your Children* (Tucson: Arizona Department of Education), 39.

19. Miller, "Know Your Children," 42.

20. Miller, "Know Your Children," 42-3.

Chapter Eight: Music Styles in Our American Culture

1. Janet Podell, ed., *Rock Music in America* (New York: H. W. Wilson Co., 1987), 18.

2. Podell, *Rock Music in America,* 13.

3. Al Menconi, with Dave Hart, *Today's Music: A Window to Your Child's Soul* (Elgin, Ill.: David C. Cook, 1990), 70.

4. Menconi with Hart, *Today's Music,* 68.

5. Menconi with Hart, *Today's Music,* 68, footnote.

6. Lawrence A. Stanley, ed., *Rap and Lyrics* (New York: Penguin Books, 1992), xv-xvi, footnote.

7. Chuck Colson, "Can We Redeem Popular Culture?" *Breakpoint,* June 1993, 17.

Chapter Nine: Music in Our Spiritual Lives

1. Gilbert Chase, *America's Music* (New York: McGraw-Hill, 1966), 6.
2. Chase, *America's Music,* 7.
3. Chase, *America's Music,* 20.
4. Chase, *America's Music,* 50-2.
5. Chase, *America's Music,* 51.
6. Al Menconi, *Media Update* 12, no. 2 (1994): 7.
7. Jane Stuart Smith and Betty Carlson, *Favorite Women Hymn Writers* (Wheaton, Ill.: Crossway, 1990), 40-3.
8. Smith and Carlson, *Favorite Women Hymn Writers,* 42.

Appendix A: A Guide to Preschool Musical Instruction

1. Shinichi Suzuki, *Nurtured by Love: A New Approach to Education.* (Athens, Ohio: Ability Development Press, 1987), 51.

About the Author

Cheri Fuller is an educator, speaker, mother of three grown children, lifelong music lover, and an Gold Medallion Award–winning author of twenty-nine books, including *When Mothers Pray, Unlocking Your Child's Learning Potential, Opening Your Child's Nine Learning Windows,* and *Opening Your Child's Spiritual Windows.* Hundreds of her articles on children, learning, and family life have been featured in magazines such as *Focus on the Family, ParentLife, Moody Monthly, Child,* and *Family Circle.* Her syndicated weekly Internet column ("Mothering by Heart"), books, articles, and messages provide practical and creative ideas for moms in the United States and around the world. Fuller and her family live in Oklahoma.

To contact Cheri Fuller regarding speaking engagements or her other books on family and children, visit her Web site at www.cherifuller.com.